Bill Hall

Bruce McNeal

John Lynch

"Grace—an exquisite word carrying the power of God for new covenant transformation. But that power depends on seeing all the dimensions of grace. The vulnerability of the authors, life stories of grace people, and the careful attention to theological foundation make *TrueFaced* a book to treasure. As you read with your heart and your life, you'll enter into the joy of your salvation!"

—GERRY BRESHEARS, PH.D., professor of theology, Western Seminary, Portland, Oregon

"Integrity, the consistency between inner life and outward life, is the essential character trait of a leader. The authors, by stripping away the false outward masks that hide the inner life, are stressing an essential feature of integrity. May many enter into *The Room of Grace* they describe."

—DR. J. ROBERT CLINTON, professor of leadership, Fuller Theological Seminary

"Make this the very next book you read. Rarely does a new work address issues that speak so deeply to the heart. *TrueFaced* is an outstanding, truly life-changing book."

—LUIS PALAU, evangelist and broadcaster; author, *Stop Pretending* (Cook)

"Masking the truth about yourself benefits no one—most significantly, you. Come clean, confess honestly, hope unswervingly, and begin living a grace-faced life! This book will help you reach that trustworthy goal."

—DR. STEPHEN A. MACCHIA, founder and president, Leadership Transformations, Inc.; author, *Becoming a Healthy Church* and *Becoming A Healthy Church Workbook*

"*TrueFaced* is a compelling invitation to pursue authenticity. This is a wonderful, liberating book full of truths that will encourage all of us to be and reveal who we really are—the people God made us to be. What a powerfully relevant message for our time!"

—DR. CRAWFORD W. LORITTS JR., author, speaker, radio host; associate director, Campus Crusade for Christ, U.S.

"*TrueFaced* helped me to continue the important journey in learning to live based on who God says I am. As I read, I was forced to lay down the book and ask myself some hard questions. It took me to places of honesty that were uncomfortable, but I emerged cleansed, ready to rest in God's love and assurance."

—BILL HULL, author, *Jesus Christ Disciple Maker,*
The Disciple-Making Pastor, and *The Disciple-Making Church*

"While actors are at their best when they are lost in the role and are not themselves, people are at their best when they confront the illusion of the role and are themselves. By exposing the futility of masks and the power in grace, *TrueFaced* is an invitation to understand the true meaning of 'being oneself.'"

—DR. ROD K. WILSON, president, Regent College, Vancouver, Canada

"This book is like a miraculous mirror—it shows us our self-imposed mask of hypocrisy and how to replace it with our true identity in Christ."

—HENRY W. HOLLOMAN, professor of systematic theology,
Talbot School of Theology, Biola University; author, *The Forgotten Blessing*

"The principles taught in *TrueFaced* will help you, as they have me, in discovering the freedom of trusting God with who you are while providing authenticity in your relationships with God and others. I will use *TrueFaced* as a guide in helping people grow in trust and spiritual maturity as they embrace God's liberating grace."

—COMMISSIONER LAWRENCE R. MORETZ, The Salvation Army, New York

"Leadership Catalyst portrays authenticity as the key to open our hearts to the transforming work of the Holy Spirit. Thrall, McNicol, and Lynch challenged me to embrace more fully the experience of love so I would be safe to strip away my masks of self protection. Taken seriously and prayerfully, you will not be left unchanged."

—JUDY TENELSHOF, PH.D., associate professor and director of the Intentional Character Development Program at Talbot School of Theology, Biola University

"This book is for Christians who seek to be authentic in their walk with Christ and with others. If you don't see yourself all too clearly in the engaging stories, then you might in response to the penetrating questions. By the time you finish, you will look more to love and grace than ever before."

—ROBERT C. ANDRINGA, PH.D., president,
Council for Christian Colleges & Universities

TrueFaced

Trust God and Others with Who You Really Are

Bill Thrall
Bruce McNicol
John Lynch

NAVPRESS®

BRINGING TRUTH TO LIFE

OUR GUARANTEE TO YOU

We believe so strongly in the message of our books that we are making this quality guarantee to you. If for any reason you are disappointed with the content of this book, return the title page to us with your name and address and we will refund to you the list price of the book. To help us serve you better, please briefly describe why you were disappointed. Mail your refund request to: NavPress, P.O. Box 35002, Colorado Springs, CO 80935.

NavPress
P.O. Box 35001
Colorado Springs, Colorado 80935

The Navigators is an international Christian organization. Our mission is to reach, disciple, and equip people to know Christ and to make Him known through successive generations. We envision multitudes of diverse people in the United States and every other nation who have a passionate love for Christ, live a lifestyle of sharing Christ's love, and multiply spiritual laborers among those without Christ.

NavPress is the publishing ministry of The Navigators. NavPress publications help believers learn biblical truth and apply what they learn to their lives and ministries. Our mission is to stimulate spiritual formation among our readers.

ISBN 1-57683-446-8

Cover Design: David Carlson Design
Cover Images: Digital Vision and PhotoDisc
Creative Team: Dan Rich, Liz Heaney, Greg Clouse, Darla Hightower, Glynese Northam

Some of the anecdotal illustrations in this book are true to life and are included with the permission of the persons involved. All other illustrations are composites of real situations, and any resemblance to people living or dead is coincidental.

Unless otherwise identified, all Scripture quotations in this publication are taken from the HOLY BIBLE: NEW INTERNATIONAL VERSION® (NIV®). Copyright © 1973, 1978, 1984 by International Bible Society. Used by permission of Zondervan Publishing House. All rights reserved. Other versions used include: the New American Standard Bible (NASB), © The Lockman Foundation 1960, 1962, 1963, 1968, 1971, 1972, 1973, 1975, 1977; and THE MESSAGE (MSG). Copyright © 1993, 1994, 1995, 1996, 2000, 2001, 2002. Used by permission of NavPress Publishing Group.

Thrall, Bill.
  Truefaced : trust God and others with who you really are / Bill Thrall, Bruce McNicol, John Lynch.
      p. cm.
Includes bibliographical references.
  ISBN 1-57683-446-8
  1. Faith. 2. Trust. I. McNicol, Bruce. II. Lynch, John. III. Title.
  BV4637.T53 2003
  234'.23--dc22
                                    2003014818

Printed in the United States of America

1 2 3 4 5 6 7 8 9 10 / 07 06 05 04 03

FOR A FREE CATALOG OF
NAVPRESS BOOKS & BIBLE STUDIES,
CALL 1-800-366-7788 (USA)
OR 1-416-499-4615 (CANADA)

Dedication

Dedicated to all those
who keep taking the immense and sacred gamble
of trusting God and others with themselves—
enjoying the astonishing ride of living TrueFaced.

Other Books by Bill Thrall and Bruce McNicol

The Ascent of a Leader

Beyond Your Best

Contents

CHAPTER ONE

Keeping Up Appearances

God hath given you one face, and you make yourselves another.
—Shakespeare, *Hamlet*

John fashioned an elaborate mask shortly after he graduated from Arizona State University in 1975. He hadn't given much thought about his future; he had just assumed it would come knocking at his door.

As May neared, his classmates started telling him about their soon-to-be-launched careers in companies such as IBM, Xerox, and Fidelity Mutual. His friends had secured real, actual careers—complete with salaries and benefits! After bragging about their bright futures, his class-mates would inevitably ask, "So, how about you, John? What field are you going into?"

"Well . . . I'm . . . uh . . . keeping my options open. I've got a lot of brands in the fire. I don't want to bite at the first thing to come along."

In truth, John had nothing in the fire, but admitting that felt way too risky. So he made two significant decisions. First, without telling any-one, he moved to Isla Vista, a small beach town near Santa Barbara,

California—a town where no one knew him and where those who did couldn't find him.

Second, he wrote to everyone he knew and told them, "Hey, I found a gig in Isla Vista. I can't believe it! I'm the featured weekend comedy act at a nightclub named Borsody's. I've worked up a bunch of new bits, local kinds of stuff. Just a couple of Saturdays ago a talent guy asked the manager if he could use me a couple nights in L.A.! Well, stay in touch. I'll write more later. I've gotta work on tonight's show."

In truth, Isla Vista did have a nightclub named Borsody's. John just made up a few of the surrounding details.

With that letter, John fashioned a mask that he thought would protect him from his friends' pity. The trouble is, once we put on a mask, we have a hard time taking it off. John kept that particular mask on for four and a half years! It had become his identity.

After a while the mask began to deceive even him. The lie rolled off of his tongue so easily that he began to believe it was part of his history—that he actually had been a comedian at Borsody's! When he describes that time in his life, John says, "I could see the smoke-filled room and the hurricane lamps at each table. I could see the light spilling onto a stage with a stool and a mike that sent my voice out into a dark sea of smiling faces. I could hear the audience's laughter and smell the beer. Now that's a mask!"

Unknown to him, John's mask was actually as thin as sketch paper. People could see right through it. Years later, he asked a few of his friends, "Did you believe me? Did you wonder if I actually was doing stand-up comedy?"

One of his best friends told him, "We never talked much about it. We just loved you. We figured that if it weren't true, it probably wouldn't help for us to blow your cover. Yeah, I guess I never really thought you were doing stand-up."

Wow! John had told himself that he had on wonderful, hip clothes: "I thought my friends were proud of me. I thought they believed I was somebody significant and famous. What a waste of energy and soul. The papier-mâché mask I thought would protect me by covering up the truth didn't. In fact, it had the opposite effect—it caused me to be the object of my friends' pity. If only I had just waited tables."

Some of us reading this might be thinking, *Whew! I'm glad I'm not like John. Imagine, lying to people about who you are! Making up stories and almost believing them yourself! That's messed up!*

It's true. Pretending to be someone you are not *is* messed up . . . messed up like the president of the United States Olympic Committee Sandy Baldwin, who suddenly lost her position for lying on her resume about her education. Or messed up like Philippine President Joseph Ejercito Estrada, who banked on macho charisma and pro-poor platforms while breaking the law "like clockwork." Estrada held millions in illicit funds through a network of hidden bank accounts. Or messed up like Alabama District Judge Jack Montgomery, who, under cover of the justice system, extorted bribes from defendants. Or like George O'Leary, who lied on his resume about his education and lost his new football coaching job at Notre Dame. Or like Tom Collen, whose resume "errors" cost him his new job as Vanderbilt's women's basketball coach. Or like

Martin Frankel, the financier who took control of seven U.S. insurance companies and embezzled over 200 million dollars before fleeing to Rome in a private jet. Or messed up like, um, well, like King Saul when he said, "I did obey God."[1]

Some of us might assume that once John became a Christian, he never again put on a mask. But we would be wrong. Since the day he came to Christ, John has put on more masks than an actor in a traveling Kabuki theater group. In fact, every time he retreats from trusting Jesus, a Pandora's box opens, and John is tempted again to put on a mask. Why? Because he's frightened at what he sees inside himself.[2] He doesn't want to reveal his true face.

If this shocks us, it shouldn't . . . not if we are being honest.

Great Mechanism for Theater . . .

The ancient Greeks loved their theater. It was the Broadway of the Appian Way. But their immense outdoor amphitheaters had some built-in problems. People in the back row could not see the actors' faces, let alone their expressions. So some director came up with the idea of having the actors deliver their lines from behind giant masks.

All the actors held a pole that carried an enormous papier-mâché mask that portrayed their predominant nature—good or evil. The mask was always a caricature—an overdone, generalized, or idealized portrayal. If the playwright wanted to show that a character had changed during the play, that actor's mask was traded for another. But the actors never revealed their true faces. Throughout the play, they all acted out their roles behind a façade. These performers were not called actors, but hypocrites, literally, "one who wears a mask."[3] A hypocrite was one who continually wore masks and whose face the audience never saw.

A great mechanism for ancient Greek theater. A tragic mechanism for people who hunger to be known and loved in the light of day.

The Masks We Wear

We are all performers, and like the actors in ancient Greece, we don't show our true faces. Because of sin, we've lost confidence that we will always please our audience, so we feel compelled to hide and put on a mask.

We have dozens of masks in our wardrobes, including:

- The "happy" mask
- The "I'm better than most" mask
- The "I'm very together" mask
- The "I'm a victim of others" mask
- The "I don't care" mask
- The "I am self-sufficient" mask
- The "I'm very important" mask
- The "I'm competent enough to not need love" mask
- The "I'm the expert" mask
- The "I am a theologically trained professional" mask
- The "I'm not hurt" mask

- The "I have the answers" mask
- The "I am independent" mask
- The "I am cool" mask

Do you recognize any of these?

The Choice to Wear a Mask

People wear masks for all sorts of reasons. Some of us opt for a mask because we fear we might not be accepted or, worse, that we may be viewed as unworthy of acceptance because we have *already* proven ourselves unacceptable. Perhaps we wear a mask because we fear that others won't protect us and might leave us feeling naked and alone. Or we fear that others *will* protect us, but our protection will come at the price of their control.

Bruce feels threatened when a person in a key relationship doubts his motives or trustworthiness. He instinctively withdraws from that person by putting on an "I don't really care" mask. Bill dons an "I'm not hurt" mask when he feels insecure and fears being abandoned. John puts on the "I am self-sufficient" mask any time he fears someone's pity.

A large percentage of people have done something similar to what John did when he made up the story about his employment at Borsody's. Many of us are hurting. We harbor painful junk that is eating us alive. And we live in a "family" that sends this unspoken message: "I prefer that you be who I want you to be rather than who you are, if it's all the same to you." So when things break down in our gig, the mask goes on and the charade begins—and everyone, *everyone,* loses.

A predictable pattern plays itself out: Some issue or pain overwhelms our hearts and we don't know how to help ourselves. We feel alone because those around us don't seem to struggle like we do, and we begin to wonder, *What's wrong with me? Why am I the only one who can't seem to get it together?* We fear exposure because we have lost confidence that we or anyone else, God included, can help us.[4] Gradually we lose all hope that we can change or be "fixed." So we cover up. We put on a mask and begin bluffing.

Most of us are in one of three groups: those living in the Land of "Doing Just Fine," those searching for the next "new" technique, or those who wear pedigreed masks.

The Land of "Doing Just Fine"

Those of us who live in the Land of "Doing Just Fine" are surrounded by nicely scrubbed people who smile broadly and shake each others' hand firmly. Our conversations go something like this:

"Hi, Milo. How ya doin'?"

"Doin' fine, Mitch. Yourself?"

"Fine, Milo. Fine. Couldn't be finer. Fine day, eh?"

"Fine indeed, Milo. Oh, hi, Mildred. How ya doin'?"

"Well, hello, Mitch. I'm doin' fine, considering the circumstances. Just fine. Fine day we're having."

"Yes, it is Mildred. Fine as fine can be. How's that husband of yours?"

"Well, Mitch, he's doin' fine too. Whole family's doin' just fine. Can't complain. Yep, I just spoke to Mrs. Sanderson and she told me that she was doing fine, but she had it on reliable information that several other unnamed families were *not* doing fine. She asked that I not share that publicly, but I tell you, only so you might pray more effectively."

"Well, that's fine with me, Mildred. At least we're fine . . . just fine."

The time has come for those of us who say we are "doin' just fine" to acknowledge the truth: We are not fine, not fine at all. We're hurting. We're lonely, confused, and frightened. We are convinced there is no real help for our issues and that the best thing we can do is to hide our true identities. It's time to admit what we are really thinking: *You have no idea who I am. Nobody knows who I am. Nobody. Not even my spouse. I'm surrounded by friends and family, but they don't know me. Every time I enter a room, it's with a persona as big as I am. I posture and position and pontificate. I can make small talk. I can even enter into meaningful, deep, theological discussion. But the person you see is made up on the run, while the real me frantically operates the levers from behind a mask. I leave almost every encounter desperately alone and feeling deeply unknown.*

The "doing just fine" masquerade paints a deeply dishonest caricature of what it means to be a follower of Jesus. Ironic, isn't it? We in the body of Christ are supposed to have the answers that can free us of hidden pain and unresolved junk, but we choose instead to pretend our lives are something they are not. The risk of rejection and alienation is too great, and so we are unwilling to break the code of silence.

If we could take off our masks, many in this group would say, "I'm tired . . . *really* tired. I'm weary of hurting and weary of dragging myself one more time through the same futile hoops I've tried hundreds of times before. I feel betrayed—betrayed by what I have been taught, betrayed by my own behavior, and betrayed by my community of faith. (Everyone there seems to be doing 'just fine.')[5] And most of all, I feel betrayed by God himself."

Still Searching for the Next "New" Technique

Those of us who make up this next group go from book to book, seminar to seminar, church to church looking for the next new technique that promises to help change us. Those in this group have admitted that life isn't "just fine." Our frustration permeates our thoughts: *Life isn't working for me. I've tried to honor the life I thought I was supposed to live, but it's not paying off like I thought it would. Give me something I can jam into my current game plan that will fix me without too much pain and change.*

But like dieters on their eleventh "new plan," the masqueraders in this group grow increasingly more disillusioned and skeptical. We have been putting bailing wire on the issues of our lives. And we know it. There *must* be an answer. There *has* to be. The God we've trusted would never just play with our heads . . . would he? We have convinced ourselves that there are answers, but we're befuddled that we can't find them. We wrestle with the whisperings of what Dr. Larry Crabb calls the three-headed dragon, who sounds more like a friend dropping in for supper:

Find a way to get on top of life. . . . Have you been to the latest conference on the spiritual life? Perhaps you should read the best-selling book that promises to unveil the secret of a happy family. There's a new therapist in town who seems to be helping a lot of people move beyond their depression into a much more satisfying life. And prayer. There are some intriguing new approaches you might want to consider. They seem to work.[6]

But our life is not getting better and we are beginning to think, *What's wrong with me? Nothing I try works. Maybe, after what I've done, I don't deserve answers. After all, others seem to figure out this stuff, but I am not changing. Nothing seems to be getting me to the abundant life that I'm supposed to be experiencing. Nothing I do seems to make any difference.*

We read about concepts and strategies that have promised to change us, but we remain ultimately unchanged . . . and we know it . . . and we fear that others are beginning to know it. Oh, we've learned a new vocabulary and can rearrange the lawn furniture of our behaviors, but deep inside, we know we're no different. We believe that if others could spend a moment inside of us they would be disgusted by what they discover. We're appalled because we have already discovered it. And we are deeply afraid that they will discover the truth about us. So we pretend to be someone we are not. And this hidden, pretend person disgusts us most.

We're starting to lose all hope that we *can* change. We suspect that what we are missing is totally hidden from our understanding or ability to fix. We feel stuck in our deep insecurity and shame. So, we continue to bluff. We marshal all of our best appearances and smile a lot.

At this point, some of us are likely thinking, *What's WRONG with these people? Why can't they get their act together?* If so, we are part of the third group.

The Pedigreed Mask

We are the "together" folk, the postcard family: well-educated, well-heeled, well-groomed, well-assured . . . and, well, a lot of work for the rest of us.

Quite frankly, our life doesn't really have this messy stuff in it. It all just slides right off. Our home and family and hobbies are almost as perfect as we are. We don't need help or answers; we *are* help and answers. Always well stocked with teaching for others, we have little need of anyone to teach us. It is all working for us. We are the standard by which the industry is judged. (Somebody has to be the benchmark of how Christians are supposed to look. It might as well be us.) We are right, and if only others could learn from us, they would be able to get on with their little lives. Our behavior is airtight and we know we are morally superior. We are not vulnerable. We don't need to be, for we are self-sufficient.[7]

If there is a higher order in the Christian community, we are in it. We intimidate others, but we know it's because they are jealous. If they had our self-determination and discipline they wouldn't have to be intimidated. If they have an issue with us, well, then it's all about them. Our goal is to get around them, get rid of them, or get over them.

This book may be for those of us in this group most of all, for we are in desperate need. We deny that we even wear a mask, but the truth about us is this: Those who know us best wish they could tell us that, while our resume is impressive, our mask is coming apart. They long to get past our mask so that they could love us and know us and know our love, but we have kept them at such a distance that they have given up. We are truly the emperor wearing no clothes.

The High Cost of Mask-Wearing

We pay a very high price when we choose to don a mask. For one thing, no one—not even those we love—ever gets to see our face. Even more tragic, our mask-wearing has an incredibly negative impact on those we influence. When we don a mask, we convince others that:

- They too must form a mask.
- They too must present an idealized person.
- They too must hide what is true about themselves.
- New life in Christ doesn't work.
- It is better to be unknown than to risk rejection.
- Self-protection is their only hope.

When we don a mask, we teach others:

- To live in guarded fear.
- To live a life of comparison, envy, and jealousy.
- To trade vulnerability for the veneer of safety.

So, we're not just actors. We are also directors in a badly styled play, teaching those we love how to pose and masquerade, memorize fake lines, rehearse expressions, and produce false tears on command.

Sadly, cruelly, our masks deceive us into believing that we can hide our true selves. Not so. In time, others can usually see what we're trying to hide. No matter how beautifully formed, our masks eventually present us as tragic figures . . . because masks always crack.

The Great Denial

Perhaps you are thinking, *This can't be me they're talking about. The mask came off when I became a Christian and I have no reason to put on another one!*

How we wish that all of us—those who know Jesus and those simply curious about him—could give ourselves permission to ask throughout this book, "Could this be *me* they're describing? What if these things were actually true about *me*?"

You see, *mask-wearing is sometimes even more pronounced in Christians.* Youch! We pretend something is true in our lives that our experience denies. Such pretending covers the real us. That pretending may be fueled by a sincere desire to want to make God look good by having our act together. He has no need for such help from us, but we think it is our obligation, nonetheless. So, we cover our dirty laundry and think we're doing the right thing by "modeling" to the world how well God improves the lives of Christians. Instead, we usually just come off as weird, stiffly religious, proud, and working way too hard.

A word of warning before we go any further: like a flu shot, the next few chapters may make you feel worse before you feel better. You may be tempted to skip ahead to the chapters that give answers that free the heart to joy. Don't do that. All of us need to be able to recognize our patterns of hiding. We need to understand how wearing a mask has affected our relationships and frustrated our maturing and influence. Do not skip ahead. Do not jam this fresh look at timeless truth into old boxes. Please don't presume you already get this stuff, or you'll blissfully skip through this book and maybe miss God's call to your heart.

The Wonderful News

We named this book *TrueFaced* for a couple of reasons. First, we wanted to communicate that almost all of us, at some time, resort to appearances, to mask-wearing—you are not some freak of nature if you see yourself in these chapters. And we wanted to point out that eventually our masks always begin to crack.

This is wonderful news.

"What?" you ask with high-pitched incredulity. "I've worked all my adult life to keep my mask from cracking. How could that possibly be anything but the worst news?"

Well, imagine if the mask didn't crack. If our masks succeeded in their attempts at self-protection, thus keeping us from love, trust, authenticity, and freedom, then we might go our entire lives missing out on what we were created for. So God allows our masks to crack and chip and distort because he loves us so much.

Which brings us to the second reason for the book's title. In this book we present truths that can help you begin, by God's grace, to reveal your true face. It's a really cool face. God made it and can't wait to see his reflection in it. Those who love you can't wait to see it either. As a friend has said when describing her life behind the mask, "The trouble with papier-mâché is that it doesn't reflect."

Maybe you are beginning to suspect that your mask has a crack. Maybe you are ready to ask some hard questions. Welcome aboard, friend. It is a journey many of us are walking.

When we admit that the old answers don't work anymore, we stop reading authors with nice-sounding platitudes and slogans, and we become hungry for books that don't deny pain or tell you to keep trying what hasn't worked before. Alongside of others in a fragile community of grace, the three of us who wrote this book are learning these truths. We are on the same journey; hungry for the promises of this life Jesus offered and still offers.

Let's look for ourselves in these next *three* chapters, and call out to the living God, "Father, is this me they're describing? Can you show me a way out of this maze? It's all I've ever known. I know you long for it to be different between you and me. I know you long for my life to count and for me to experience joy, fulfillment, and purpose. I have nothing to lose but a life that wasn't working anyway. Come reveal to me my true face, reflecting yours."

DID YOU DISCOVER?

- We've lost our confidence that we will always please our audience, so we feel compelled to hide and put on a mask.

- There are dozens of masks in the wardrobe from which to choose.

- Those who know us best wish they could tell us that our mask is coming apart.

- Pretending to have our act together may be fueled by a sincere desire to make God look good.

- Most of us fall into one of three groups: those who pretend things are just fine, those searching for new techniques to get better, and those who wear "pedigreed masks."

- The costs of wearing masks are enormous, both for ourselves and those we influence.

- Mask-wearing is sometimes even more pronounced in Christians than in those still seeking Christ.

- The next three chapters, like a flu shot, may make us feel worse before we get better.

- God wants to see his reflection in our faces, but the trouble with papier-mâché is that it doesn't reflect.

- This book is named *TrueFaced* because we all resort to appearances and struggle to find our true faces, and second, because a wonderful opportunity for healing and maturing eventually occurs—our masks begin to crack.

CHAPTER TWO

How Did This Happen?

"There is a face that we hide
Till the nighttime appears,
And what's hiding inside,
Behind all of our fears,
Is our true self
Locked inside the façade!"
—Jekyll and Hyde

☰ Over time, most of us notice that our struggles are not going away. In fact, we have to paste more and more layers on our mask just to hold it together. Our real emotions—which are threatening and inappropriate—scare us. So we say things we don't believe and pretend to like things we dislike. Some of us have become a human time bomb—resentful and guarded and ready to blow. We need a lot of down time so we can be alone, free from pretending.

Those around us know something's wrong. Some worry that it might have something to do with the masks *they're* wearing. Others have stopped trying to work through any problems or concerns they have with us; they have learned not to bring up things that trigger us to overreact. "Don't try to talk to him about. . . ." "Don't ask her about. . . ."

"Don't suggest. . . ." Eventually people stop risking intimacy with us. They tiptoe around us. "He's too thorny, too unsafe, too erratic." "She's too defensive, too unpredictable."

Most of us saw ourselves somewhere in the last chapter. Most of us will admit, "I know I wear masks. Sometimes I feel like I'm working off a prepared script. I'll say the most trite-sounding things in order to cover my real feelings. I don't really like this about me, but I have no idea how to take my masks off. If I did, I don't think I would have gotten into this mess."

But if asked where all this junk comes from, most of us couldn't answer. *Most of us are in the dark about how we got like this.* We blame our actions on circumstances or the pressure we're under. "I must be going through menopause or a mid-life crisis," we say. And that makes sense . . . until we are reminded that we aren't yet forty!

One of the really good gifts we could receive would be the ability to see where we are and how we got there. We need to see ourselves in our story, to see what causes and nurtures the responses that trip us up. We must see that our controlling behavior isn't a response to something happening in the present. It was triggered by some sin in the past that never got resolved. If we can begin to understand the phases of unresolved sin and discover what is happening to us, we may no longer react to life like lemmings heading for a cliff.

In this chapter we hope to help you begin doing just that. It's meant to be used as a diagnostic tool that can tell you where the problem is and what may have caused it.

What Unresolved Sin Does to the Heart

No car ever started moving simply because someone turned a key. The key triggered something, which caused something else to fire, which forced some other something to rotate, eventually starting the engine.

In a similar way, an unresolved act of sin can trigger a predictable and uncompromising three-phase process:

Act of Sin → Involuntary Response → Inevitable Effect

Sin sets the ball in motion. Someone sins against us or we sin against someone else, and that *act of sin* evokes within us an *involuntary response*.[1] We don't have to work at producing these responses. They are automatic.

If we do the sinning, our involuntary response is called *guilt*.[2] If someone else sins against us, our involuntary response is called *hurt*.[3] God designed these two responses to tell us that something wrong has happened—something just got fractured and needs healing.

However, many of us cover up our guilt or hurt because we don't know what to do with our responses. If we hide or try to override our guilt or hurt—if we do not move toward resolution—life gets very bad in a hurry. Our *involuntary responses* will progress to *inevitable effects*, unleashing a new depth of pain, inner turmoil, and mask-wearing.

Most of us never tie together the *act of sin*, the *involuntary responses*, and the *inevitable effects*. We are not aware of the chain reaction. We only know we are carrying feelings, thoughts, and behaviors we can't figure out and feel a need to mask. But our futile disguise simply tells others we have problems. They have no more idea than we do about why we're acting so oddly. They just pity us. Or talk about us. Or they find socially acceptable ways to keep their distance. We're like a tourist trying to impress his waiter by bluffing fluency in another language, unaware that instead of medallions of lamb he just ordered a dish of metal fasteners. He unwittingly becomes the subject of much ridicule and mockery back in the kitchen.

Wouldn't it be great to discover how to stop this three-phase chain reaction? Wouldn't it be awesome to discover how our cracking mask could actually be removed to expose the wonderful face God has always wanted to reveal? Wouldn't it be incredibly fantastic to have that kind of hope?

Hope begins by understanding this critical point: Both the one who sins and the one sinned against have an *involuntary heart response* to an *act of sin*.

- In the one who sins, the effect is *guilt*.
- In the one who is sinned against, the effect is *hurt*.

In the One Who Sins: Guilt

Guilt is a good thing. God has graciously etched a benchmark in our hearts. A standard. God calls it a conscience.[4] It roars to life in order to make us aware of sin we have committed.

When we do something wrong, we feel guilt, at least initially. Guilt yells, "Hey pal, pay attention to this. If you think guilt feels lousy, just try to ignore it and see what follows!" If we don't recognize the purpose of the guilt—to prompt us to resolve our sin—we may just forget to deal with our sin. Eventually the incident will fade from our memory and our guilt loses its sharp edge. We would rather ignore our sin than acknowledge that we did something wrong, so we stuff the guilt we feel.

But here's what happens. In stuffing our guilt, we avoid admitting that what we did deeply harmed and impacted another. Our sin *hurt* someone. The decision to ignore our sin creates *unresolved sin*, which is like an undiagnosed disease that quietly spreads poison throughout our bloodstream. We may recognize we don't have the energy we used to have, but we blame this on something or someone else and fail to recognize that an invisible, inner enemy drains our energy and joy. This destructive sequence occurs because, even though we tried to bury it, our unresolved sin remains very much alive.

When an act of known sin remains unresolved, it causes *a nagging sense in the heart that doesn't go away*. To resolve this sin, we need to access God's resources for dealing with what we know we have done and with what our actions have done to others. Of course, resolving a sin doesn't mean we'll never struggle with it again. It only means we've stopped its present path of destruction and are living in health. It means we're addressing a particular known act of sin, openly and specifically, in a safe environment. This is not a process that creates a search for what we do not know. This is a process that deals with known sin.

Many of us avoid dealing with how our sin affects others because we can't face the reality of what it says about us. "I can't be known as a person who does that kind of thing." Or perhaps we are not convinced God can help or heal us. Like plaque, unresolved sin builds up. Eventually we have so much junk in our lives that we're convinced God can barely tolerate us. Left unresolved, one act of sin lays the groundwork for serious relational breakdowns. There's a dried out kettle of spoiled herring for you.

In the One Sinned Against: Hurt

Meanwhile, the one who sustains the impact of sin experiences hurt or violation.

Nothing in us enables us to absorb the sin done against us and the hurt that follows. Nothing. This makes most of us want to scream, "But that isn't fair. I was not the one who sinned." And we're right. It is not fair. Sin is not fair. But, when we are sinned against and we don't know how to resolve that sin, *it will always ignite the nature of the sin already in us.* We, the hurt ones, now give ourselves permission to act out sinfully.[5] Twisted, isn't it?

This hurt is also a very good thing. God made us to feel hurt so that we would go to him for healing. But that's a pretty fragile thing to do—to admit that we feel hurt. It feels like we are giving in to our offender—letting him or her off the hook. And sometimes we were hurt at such a young age that we didn't even understand that someone had sinned against us. So instead of going to God, we tell ourselves, "I'll be fine. I just need to move on. I'm fine . . . really." So, we walk on, unconsciously adding to the unresolved hurt of dozens of other sins committed against us. Meanwhile, we don't know why we feel so angry, depressed, and bitter.

It's as if we've wrenched our back, wrenched it for the fourth time over the last three months. We try to convince ourselves that the problem can be solved with a bag of ice cubes. After a couple of days, the pain subsides. Other than occasional stiffness, we basically just forget about it. We figure we've dodged the bullet of the chiropractor. Then one day we drop our keys in the Wal-Mart parking lot. And as we bend down to pick them up, we suddenly fall to our knees with a yelp. Hunched over, we look to passersby like a deeply devout woman suddenly moved to pray. Several high-school kids see us and help us back into our car. One of them cautions the others to be careful because "older people's bones are more brittle." Suddenly, the tiniest wrong move has made us walk like one of the early figures on an evolutionary wall chart. We require two days of bed rest, watching infomercials about basting ovens.

The good news is that we can stop the damage of an *act of sin* done against us at any time by applying God's resources and power to resolve that sin. Remember, this can be a place of hope. But if we don't access God's resources, the devastating pattern continues.

How Guilt and Hurt Mutate

When we trust our own ideas about how to handle our guilt or hurt, we allow something much worse to be released in us. Suddenly, our guilt or hurt morphs into half a dozen or more ugly *inevitable effects*. Guilt and hurt turn into *shame, blame, fear, denial*, and *anger*. Something under our own roof begins to destroy us! How sad is *that*?

This means that if we don't resolve the sin that caused us to feel guilt or hurt, it will inflame sin within us—even if the sin was not initially ours. Guilt or hurt, those wonderful God-given gifts, have mutated into *inevitable effects* that have no purpose but to harm us. When too much pressure on a dam produces a crack, it must be sealed or the water behind the dam inevitably floods the village below. Similarly, our choice to go our own way at the *involuntary response* phase propels us into the uncontrollable and unstoppable—the *inevitable effects*.

This three-phase process plays out in every person, even those who don't claim to follow Christ. The only real difference between this group and Christ followers is the hope of a solution. But if we, as Christians, refuse that hope, we lay ourselves open to an endless variety of counterfeits that promise relief: We start trusting techniques, conscience-numbing medication, pop psychology, spiritual fads, and a hundred other nicely packaged weasels. Whenever we sin and don't resolve that sin, either because we don't know how or choose not to, we release an inevitable force that will drain confidence in who we really are.

Now we need a top-of-the-line mask, maybe several. We hastily snatch them up from dozens of designer options: "I'm better than most," "I'm very together," "I don't really care," "I am self-sufficient," "I'm very important," "I'm competent enough to be loved," "I am competent enough not to need love," "I have the answers," "I'm independent," or "I am cool." But all the while, our heart whispers: *You're a fake, an impostor, a loser. You always have been. You always will be. You may fool others, but I know who you are. You're a joke, the definition of hypocrite. You have no self-respect. You spent it long ago.*

A Sampling of Inevitable Effects

So now we enter a new land of coping, covering, plotting, and reacting. We view life through a destructive, self-protective grid that produces any number of *inevitable effects*, including *shame, blame, fear, denial,* and *anger.* None of these "just happen" to appear in our hearts. We invited them to grow up and make themselves right at home there. They have nothing but harm to offer us, and will do so until we run back to God's offer of healing. Until then, they shape how we see our lives.

Let's take a closer look at some of the most common and significant *inevitable effects.* Not every unresolved sin results in every effect. And we may experience two or more of these effects simultaneously from the same unresolved sin.

Shame

Unresolved guilt and hurt produce shame in us. When Adam and Eve violated God's command and then refused to take responsibility for that sin, they experienced the shame of their own nakedness. This shame, this self-perception of embarrassment and being "dirty," prompted them to fashion a mask from fig leaves to hide what was true about them.[6]

They were the first to try to give the appearance that they were someone other than who they actually were!

Thanks, Adam and Eve. Nice legacy.

Guilt makes us aware of sin and evokes in us a feeling of shame when we don't resolve that sin. And, like Adam, we instinctively fashion a mask to cover our shame. Only when we apply God's covering can we break this pattern.

Hurt makes us aware that we have been sinned against. Not all violations result in hurt, but when someone sins against us and we feel hurt, and we do not resolve that sin, we will feel demeaned and humiliated. This becomes our experience of shame. It doesn't matter that we did not commit the initial sin. Whenever we fail to access God's healing resources and power to resolve a sin—even sin committed against us—unresolved sin will inflame shame in our own hearts.

Blame

Back to the garden. Roll the film forward. The Lord confronts Adam and Eve with their actions[7] and they both humbly take the hit for the other. Yeah, right! And Al Qaeda repent of their ways and come to the United States to revitalize the Welcome Wagon program.

When God confronts Adam, Adam blames Eve. "The woman . . . she gave me from the tree, and I ate."[8] But Adam's not done. He goes right to the top—he blames God! "The woman *you* put here with me—she gave me some fruit from the tree."[9] Eve, not to be outdone, blames the serpent. It's a veritable blame fest. We're surprised that the serpent doesn't blame the tree! "Someone else must be blamed for my sin." When we sin, we often try to absolve ourselves of the guilt by shifting the blame to another. There is no order to these *inevitable effects*: We can blame others because we feel shame or we can feel shame because of blame.

When we are sinned *against,* we frequently do something similar. We begin to view ourselves as victims and develop a victim's mindset, blaming who we are on what others have done to us, or what they may do someday. We're convinced we have no choice in who we are or in who we are becoming and that we are no longer responsible for our inappropriate reactions. We are absolved of all that is wrong with us. We become the judge, jury, and warden of the universe. We are the victim of all we survey.

Fear

So God comes in the cool of the day to be with Adam and Eve after the "apple incident." But now the two have hidden from his presence. He calls out to Adam, "Where are you?" Adam responds, "I heard the sound of you in the garden, and I was afraid because I was naked; so I hid myself."[10]

How ironic: Because of his sin, Adam feared the one who'd created him, the one who loved him and sought him out. When we make God the bad guy, we almost immediately experience a lack of hope.

Fear—an *inevitable effect* of unresolved sin—creates a barrier in relationships. When we sin against others, it creates a fear within us that prompts us to hide from them. We may not hide from them physically, but we hide socially and emotionally. This cheapens our relationships because we lose the transparency that deepens the bonds of love, care, and support. We begin to speak in code, chatting about superficial, impersonal issues of life. Because they don't know what is going on within us, they can't empathize or identify with our loneliness, hurt, or discouragement. We hide behind a mask that says, "Nothing I do seems to make a difference." But we are withering inside; we are afraid.

We fear others, though they have done nothing to warrant our fear. We worry that they will discover our hidden life. We fear they will confront us with our unresolved sin. We dread their contempt. We fear that they will discover we are not as competent as they previously thought. We are afraid they will reject us or speak to others about us. We become convinced there is a club that meets regularly for the sole purpose of hurting us by our lack of invitation. Ironically, we fear the very ones God designed to love us. That is true irony—we hide from what will heal us.[11]

Those hurt by acts of sin also experience this *inevitable effect* and, out of fear, try to hide from others. Their hurt has convinced them that others cannot and should not be trusted. In addition, their hurt causes them to believe there must be something about them that gives an offender the *right* to hurt them, so they fear being known at all. They keep everyone out—even those who could love them and help them heal.

Denial

Unresolved guilt or hurt can also make us vulnerable to patterns of denial. We find no joy in admitting we are sinners—that is way too risky.

Nor do we find joy in admitting we are hurting—that also feels too risky. We already feel at the edge of other people's acceptance. We can't let another thing be added to the list, or they may reassess our worthiness for their friendship.

Denial keeps us from facing the truth about ourselves. If we are the offender, it allows us to deny that we've done anything wrong. If we are the offended, it allows us to deny that the sin done to us has affected us.

If we have unresolved guilt, our denial can range from lying about our actions to refusing to acknowledge the consequences of our act of sin on the other person. "Come on, you're making a big deal out of nothing. I *said* I was sorry!" If we have unresolved hurt, we will deny we've been hurt. Such an admission would make us too fragile, too vulnerable. So, we try to deny any pain, hurt, or violation.

As we write, all three of us are thinking of friends who live every day of their lives in this drafty dungeon called denial. We have wasted time there too. People who live in denial refuse to give permission to others to speak about the things everyone else can see. Those in denial insist that friends agree with their assessments and rewriting of history. Inside their fortress, those in denial are becoming self-vindicating judges. They are alone. And they are secretly terrified, because they know the truth of what they deny.

Anger

Anger brings a heroic sense of purpose to our guilt or our hurt. It gives us energy, explosive and unpredictable energy.

Anger that comes from guilt says, "Yeah, I did something wrong. But I'll bet if you stacked the things I've done wrong against others' failings, I'd come out smelling pretty good. I'm tired of taking the fall all the time because somebody reacted badly to something I did or said. Why is it that other people get me into these messes, but I'm the one who gets blamed? Somebody's gonna pay besides me."[12] And now, we are on our way to producing more acts of sin, leading to more guilt, breeding even more anger. Our societies are full of this kind of accumulating rage. Dallas Willard writes, "Anger and contempt are the twin scourges of the earth."[13]

Anger that comes from hurt says, "I am not at all where I want to be. I am experiencing a life I do not deserve. I was unfairly hurt. And I am deeply, deeply ticked off. I want a hearing. I want to gather support. I want to use every means and weapon I have at my disposal to make somebody, somewhere pay for the outrage done to me. If no one else is going to admit that I have been treated unfairly, including God, then I will, by myself, bring others to justice."

Many people say, "I just don't know why I get so angry." Most often they don't know because they have never traced their anger back to its root—to unresolved sin, either from hurt or guilt. They also don't know because anger is blind. It cannot see truth very well—the truth of anger's resolution. Anger has a limited and distorted perspective. It thinks, *Because I'm hurt, I must be right.* Anger holds court without evidence or witnesses and carries only the perspective of the presumed innocent party. Even if we are partially responsible for the wrong that we've experienced, our anger hides this fact.

Sharon's Story

To help us explain just how destructive this three-phase process can be, we've asked a good friend of ours, Sharon, to tell her story. It's the story of how acts of sin against her, which remained unresolved for years, played themselves out in her life.

Sharon grew up in a family well respected for its great teachers, worship leaders, and community pillars. As a young girl, she sang beautifully and played a number of instruments proficiently. Poised, attractive, intelligent, and charming, Sharon had enormous potential, drive, and passion. But as she became a young adult, every now and then Sharon would unexpectedly erupt in rage over something fairly insignificant. For the most part, friends chalked it up to the eccentricities of an unusually gifted person.

As Sharon became an adult, she gained more and more responsibilities that matched her growing proficiency. But she didn't smile as much or as easily. She found herself lashing out at her new husband and then feeling terrible for what she had done. Her angry eruptions became more frequent. Outsiders saw Sharon as a role model, but to those close to her, she was an enigma. At times she demonstrated tremendous kindness and goodness, but more and more often she was given to fits of rage, judgment, criticism, and blame. When she entered her thirties, much of Sharon's kindness was replaced with a growing air of superiority. She grew incredibly driven, and spent more and more time alone.

How did this happen? How did Sharon get so angry? What could cause these increasing displays of pain in a seemingly together person? Based on the three phases of unresolved sin, what would we expect to find beneath the surface? What *acts of sin*? What *involuntary responses* might create a mix of such competency wrapped in dysfunction? We'll let Sharon tell you herself:

I grew up attending church each time the doors were open, and I trusted Jesus as my savior as a very young girl. But what I heard in church and what I experienced at home were two very different things. My "Christian" parents sinned violently against me. My father and many other men used me sexually, and my mother knew of it. Whenever I resisted, my parents would twist Scripture by saying that children are to obey their parents "in all things."

My parents did further harm to me by repeatedly telling me I was born with the "wrong personality" and that no man would ever want to marry me because I was too strong. I knew that God had created me to be a leader, but my parents did their best to crush those qualities in my personality. They manipulated Scripture to demean the place of women in God's eyes. Their abuse and legalism wounded me deeply.

As a child I wasn't able to bring to God the *acts of sin* done against me. I couldn't even understand what was happening to me and didn't know what to do with the *involuntary responses* of hurt and guilt. Because I did not know how to resolve my hurt, a torrent of *inevitable effects* was unleashed in my life.

The sexual abuse left me with physical scars, noted by my obstetrician at my daughter's birth. Because I was just a child, I felt I must have done something to deserve the abuse, and this "false guilt" made me feel shame. I felt as if I'd become shame itself. I felt that I didn't deserve to be looked upon with anything but contempt. I was no more than raw sewage.

My shame caused me to grow up believing I was unlovable. Why else would someone violate a little girl so often? I was only worthy to be used and hated. I certainly wasn't worthy to be protected.

I also had emotional scars from years of neglect and hurt, and spiritual wounds from my deep confusion over what I read in the Bible and what I had experienced. I was desperately trying to be the "right" kind of woman. But I had no idea how I should act, because I didn't even understand who I was. But the deepest wound was my heart's lack of hope that anyone could ever love me. I had no idea what to do with the constant hurt and pain.

Of course, I had to hide the truth of my life, so I became very skilled at hiding my shame—or so I hoped. Hiding became the goal of my existence. I did everything I could to control my circumstances. I learned to change my behavior to fit the spiritual culture of wherever I was. I became very judgmental of others. I chose to feel superior to them so that I could feel better about myself. I dealt with my hurt by burying it under an intense rage. Anger made me feel in control. I felt I needed to be in control at all costs. If I felt anger, I could always blame someone or something for it. I was very good at blaming.

My self-protective behaviors gave me an illusion of safety, but they also kept me from getting my real needs met. *I had allowed the sin done to me to inflame my own sin—and I didn't know what to do about it.* I didn't trust anyone. I felt alone, unsafe, and unlovable, long after I was far from my parents' home.

Out of God's abundant grace, I got married and had two children. But I could not wear my mask twenty-four hours a day, seven days a week. I couldn't keep up the façade of the perfect, godly woman. I unleashed my anger at home, on my husband and kids. I felt hypocritical, because I wasn't the same person at home that I projected at church. I didn't want to continue pretending to be someone I wasn't.

I was finally around people who wanted me to be the person I was created to be, but I had absolutely no idea how to do it! The hurt, buried under my anger, was trying to surface and I didn't know how to go to God with it. I was bitter at my parents and my siblings. I was resentful of my husband for not meeting my needs. I was a toxic person to those closest to me.

I was everything I didn't want to be, and it caused me to feel even more unlovable. And I couldn't stop it.

We'll come back to Sharon's story in chapter seven. But for now, we can tell you that all of this has changed for Sharon in profound ways. As a result of applying many of the healing truths laid out in this book, she is now experiencing an astonishing life.

What About You?

Well, maybe it's time to put the book down again and ask:

- Have I gone down a road leading to *shame, blame, fear, denial,* and *anger*?
- Has someone close to me walked down that road without the foggiest idea how to come back home?

Don't rush over these questions. Don't be afraid to admit if you have been so needy. Look fully into the mirror and don't walk away. If you stop long enough to see yourself, the rest of this book will be cool water in a dry and weary land. God says to you, "Hello, my dear child. I've missed you. Welcome home."

⣿ DID YOU DISCOVER?

- An unresolved sin is a known sin that creates a nagging sense in the heart that doesn't go away.

- An unresolved act of sin can trigger a predictable and uncompromising three-phase process:

  Act of Sin → Involuntary Response → Inevitable Effect

- Hope begins by understanding this critical point: Both the one who sins and the one sinned against have an *involuntary response* of the heart to an *act of sin.*
    - In the one who sins, the effect is *guilt.*
    - In the one who is sinned against, the effect is *hurt.*

- The decision to ignore our sin creates *unresolved sin*, which is like an undiagnosed disease that quietly spreads poison throughout our bloodstream.

- We can stop the damage of an *act of sin* done against us at any time by applying God's resources and power to resolve that sin.

- Our choice to go our own way at the *involuntary response* phase propels us into the uncontrollable and unstoppable—the *inevitable effects.* A sampling of five:

- *Shame* can result from either unresolved guilt or unresolved hurt.
- *Blame* is used to try to absolve ourselves of the guilt caused by our sin.
- *Fear* creates barriers in relationships.
- *Denial* keeps us from facing the truth about ourselves.
- *Anger* has a limited and distorted perspective. It thinks, *Because I'm hurt, I must be right.*

CHAPTER THREE

Behind the Mask, Part One

Away, and mock the time with fairest show;
False face must hide what the false heart doth know.
—Shakespeare, *Macbeth*

$\equiv$ Each of us brings into every encounter our own personal history, temperament, personality, wounding, influences, and previously unresolved sin issues. And when we don't access God's remedy to deal with sin, those ugly, destructive *inevitable effects* join forces inside us like oily characters from a gangster movie:

(Read the following dialogue with a cheesy accent.) "Hey, Shame, look who the cat just drug in!"

"Well, I'll be, Guilt. It's Denial and his weasly little buddies, Fear and Anger! Hey, how youse guys doin'? I ain't seen youse around these parts since this sap's little tax indiscretion in '98. He tried to pass off an Acapulco fishing derby as a charitable deduction, remember? Yeah, those were the days. So whaddaya say we work together again? Workin' alone ain't much fun. I mean, what good is Denial unless Shame's hangin' around to sweeten the pot? Anger don't get much mileage without Guilt fuelin' the fire. Am I right, or am I right? Whaddaya say, guys? All of us workin' together again, for old time's sake. We could make this guy a wreck. Imagine Guilt, Denial, Fear, Anger, and Shame workin' against him. Boy, he's gonna be a lot of fun at a party. He'll be so wigged out, his hair could catch fire and he'd pretend everything's just fine. Let's get to work, boys."

It's hard to predict which inevitable effects will follow from which involuntary responses. This is not an exact science. Let's take a look at six damaging behaviors we engage in when the inevitable effects join forces inside us. There are dozens more behaviors, but in this book we'll limit our examination to the following:

1. I become highly sensitized to my own sin and judge the sin of others.
2. I lose my objectivity in a crisis and I become the issue.
3. I hide my sinful behavior and become vulnerable to more sin.
4. I am unable to be loved or to love.
5. I become susceptible to wrong life choices.
6. I attempt to control others.

In this chapter we'll examine the first three *inevitable effects*.

I Become Highly Sensitized to My Own Sin and Judge the Sin of Others

When we are unable or unwilling to resolve the sin within us, we become deeply sensitized toward our own sin . . . and others' sins. Suddenly, we become a self-appointed judge of what is wrong with other people![1] Our shame causes us to find blame in them. (This is why people often feel judged around those filled with shame.) Like Javert, the law-obsessed police officer in *Les Misérables*, we become fixated on making sure others pay for what they have done.

If our newfound sensitivity to sin gave us greater ability to solve the sin in our lives, that would be one thing, but this is not what happens. Sadly, the one with the keen sensitivity to sin is often the one without the ability to deal with that sin!

When this *inevitable effect* plays itself out in our lives, our sensitivity to our own sin and the sins of others causes us to create legalistic and controlling environments. When this is true in families, this damaging pattern can be passed on from generation to generation.

Years of directing Christian summer high-school camps gave Bruce and Bill an incredible desire to discover how to break the patterns of generational dysfunction they saw being played out over and over again in the lives of kids. They discovered that the teenagers with the greatest scars were *not* the unchurched kids, but those who came from Christian homes with intense religious control. These kids lived daily without expressed love—and it scarred their souls. They blamed the God of their parents and were unable to trust others. They had no solution for the hopelessness in their hearts. The very God who alone had answers for them was, in their minds, no answer at all.

Many of those teenagers are now adults suffering the long-lasting effects of their parents' condemnation. They continue to live in dysfunctional relationships, now victims of their own choice not to seek

God's healing. Like their parents, they hide their true faces. They live under their own legalism, and unless the pattern is broken, they too will harm the generation that follows them.

Sara was one of those campers. She came from a Christian home with a strict, legalistic father and a passive, compliant mother. Sixteen, bright, and attractive, Sara knew all the "right" answers, yet she grew up believing that she was not good enough. She saw herself as unlovable.

At camp Sara was quiet and brooding, unwilling to engage in anything to do with the Bible because her dad had used it to justify his condemnation of her. He watched her every move, anticipating and predicting her next sin. He displayed no trust in her, offered no praise. Sadly, Sara learned her father's lesson well. Today she turns to drugs and sex to numb the pain in her soul.

What a sick transfer! Those judged actually begin to believe that they *deserve* the guilt they feel or the shame they bear. People like Sara's father—those with sensitivity to sin without the power of grace to deal with that sin—will ruin the spirit and deeply violate the soul of those they claim to love and are responsible to love.

Those we influence will be affected by what is true in us, no matter how well we think we are hiding. They will bear the brunt of our sensitivity to our own sin, because they will bear our judgment. Then, shame, blame, fear, and anger combine in them to create another generation of distorted sensitivity to the sin in others. Like a bad carnival ride, no one can get off and it all just keeps making you sicker.

You mean that's why my children and those I influence begin to learn my behaviors and copy my dysfunctions? Yes. Children become what they catch from their parents. They catch our words and our actions. A mother says, "I can't believe I'm yelling at my children, just like my mother did. I promised myself I would never be like her." A father says, "I've withdrawn from intimacy in my family relationships, because I promised myself I would never use on my children the anger my father used on me." But because he never addresses the source of his anger, his withdrawal becomes a moody, passive-aggressive form of destructive anger.

And so it goes. The judgment cycle passes from generation to generation and from environment to environment.[2] It spreads, like an infectious cold, to those we love most and desire to have the greatest influence upon.

I Lose My Objectivity in a Crisis and I Become the Issue

When we put on a mask due to unresolved sin, we lose our objectivity in a crisis. Everything revolves around this subjective, distorted, and idealized picture we now have of ourselves. We react out of that warped self-portrait.

Objectivity is one of the greatest gifts parents, teachers, mentors, or spouses can bring to an assessment of someone they care about. But when we have unresolved sin issues, the pressure of a crisis only serves to fan their embers. We move from an ability to see the problem clearly to becoming the problem.

In other words, in a crisis:

- I become unable to read and evaluate the behavior, contributions, motives, and attitudes of others around me in a healthy way. I can only read them in terms of their effect on me.
- I begin to demand loyalty from those over whom I have authority, at the expense of their losing a voice.
- I manipulate circumstances to my advantage.
- I blame others with a condemnation and irritation that is distorted by subjectivity.
- I create an environment dependent on the moods I manifest.
- I cause those around me to function in fear and distrust.
- I force everyone around me to grapple with two issues: how to resolve the original issue and, now, how to handle *me!*

When this skewed behavior takes place between parents and children, devastating consequences can result. Parents who lose objectivity teach their children to react to such behavior out of fear and self-protection. The kids unconsciously think, *The person who is supposed to nurture and protect me is the one to whom I must continually react.*

When Bruce's daughter Nicole was fourteen years old, she stopped him one day as they were both passing through the family room of their home. With the boldness of a teenager who knows she's captured some insight, she said, "Dad, you've given me permission to talk with you about your life, and I just wanted to say that when you get angry, you don't get mad or blow up. That's good. But, when you get tired or frustrated, you can get really impatient with people and hurt them with your words and behaviors [meaning, *you hurt me too*]. I'm not sure what to do about that."

Nicole gave her dad a true reading of his behavior in that memorable moment. Impatience is often rooted in control issues that spring from fear and blame. Under routine circumstances, Bruce can manage this *inevitable effect*. His unresolved sin almost seems "fixed." But, in a crisis, Bruce can lose objectivity, and he can become the issue — as evidenced by his impatience.

Review the previous list, and you will see that Bruce's impatience could produce almost every one of these adverse effects in his interactions with his family, friends, and associates. Do you see how important the resolution of even one unresolved sin dysfunction can be? (Bruce may always have this impatient fault line in his life. Resolution does not mean that one becomes sinless. But biblical resolution, which we will discuss in later chapters, brings maturity, freedom, love, and influence.)

I Hide My Sinful Behavior and Become Vulnerable to More Sin

Shame, blame, denial, and fear ganged up in the life of our friend Debbie. The result: an eating disorder. It damaged her body, her relationships, her college career, and then her marriage. Ashamed of what seemed to be a problem that could not possibly be true of her, Debbie denied the reality of her sin and hid her eating disorder for several years.

This cover-up became a dark breeding ground for even more eating disorders, lying, posturing, and sad attempts at failed relationships.

No matter how deep we try to bury it, unresolved sin doesn't die. It is always alive and well, inflaming more sin.[3] Hiding creates a double whammy: It prevents us from maturing, and it makes us vulnerable to even more sin.

Environments That Promote Hiding

Certain environments encourage hiding, and therefore sin. The degree to which we wear a mask in our key relationships is the degree to which our character development will be thwarted. If we do not feel our home, church, or organization nurtures a safe place to reveal what is true about us, we will feel an incredible need to hide. We will think, *If the penalty for disclosure is the same as getting caught, why would I ever disclose my failure?* Environments without grace retain and multiply unresolved sin issues.

Wow! How many relationships are we in where the penalty for disclosing our failure is the same as getting caught? How many children have invented a polite mask to wear at home? We fashion our masks to look the way we think others would like us to appear. Meanwhile, we (and our children) are suffocating under the deceit and pain of carrying alone what we do not understand or know how to solve.

Sadly, many people create this kind of destructive environment. Bruce and Bill sat down with the leader of a Christian organization and asked what her views were on character development. Her words stunned and shocked them: "In my organization we only hire people of high character and if they demonstrate they don't have that character, we terminate them." They laughed—until they realized she wasn't kidding!

Predictably, this leader's method didn't work. Her attitude created an environment where people constantly hid their behaviors because the boss expected everyone to exhibit an airtight integrity and character. This organization went through a long period of breakdown in relationships and productivity because, as in every family, organization, or ministry, the people in it had sin issues. The company made it unsafe for them to be honest about their struggles, and so they hid them until they eventually got caught and released, or until they could no longer live with the duplicity and left. What a cruel joke.

In such an environment (especially one where sinning less is proof of godliness), almost everyone hides something. Hiding becomes an unspoken, almost unconscious way of life. The environment sucks the life out of truth and weakens it to the point where it cannot be applied. Hiddenness, fear, and rejection are such blaring sirens that they drown out everything else. (If I tell you I love you while holding a gun to your head, you'll have a very hard time believing it!)

Roles That Promote Hiding

It's not only certain environments that promote hiding; some roles do too. If we could remember this simple principle—*the more influence we have, the more we are tempted to hide our true self for fear we will lose that influence*—we might become less susceptible to the damage leaders in organizations, churches, or workplaces can cause when they wear masks.[4] We have watched and counseled leaders of associations, schools, businesses, governments, and churches who publicly condemned other leaders for their lack of integrity. Some even sued these individuals to "guard against the wolves tearing up a faithful church." Later, it came out that those who had so harshly condemned others were guilty of notable sin—deceit, theft, pornography, fraud, or molestation—all under the cover of their powerful systems. It will always be true: The greater the privilege of influence, the greater the temptation to hide.

Those who have never learned how to apply the healing Jesus brings to their lives will always hide their sin. Hiding is naturally more serious for leaders, due to their impact on many people. Numerous Christian teachers can affirm and teach the significance of the cross, the death, and the resurrection of Jesus as the fully sufficient plan of redemption. But like a food critic without the sense of smell, many in these roles have no idea how to apply their theology to who they are. Unfortunately, this gap is harder for leaders to acknowledge than for young Christ followers, because these leaders have been elevated to positions that are too valuable to them to risk exposing what is true about themselves. The masks are never thicker or slicker.

Jeff called Bill at 3:43 A.M. from a phone booth to report that his wife had kicked him out of the house. Joan had discovered pornographic literature behind some books in his study. Jeff tried to lie his way out of the situation by telling her the magazines were from a long time ago, until she pointed out the current date on them. Jeff had been deeply enmeshed in this unresolved sin for sixteen years. At first it was just when he was out of town, but recently it had become "all the time."

At this point Jeff decided to tell Joan everything. At first she could find no words to describe her hurt. Then she started screaming loudly. Next, she slapped Jeff really hard and demanded, "Get out of this house!" The extreme behavior scared Jeff. He was stunned with the horror that he had violated his wife so deeply that she resorted to violence.

Bill asked Jeff to return home, where ten minutes later Bill talked with them both. During the conversation Joan asked, "Who is this man? Is this the person I deeply trusted as my husband and father of my children? I trusted him because he appeared to live what he taught. I feel like I've been a fool."

For sixteen years, Jeff had told himself that he and God would deal with his problem privately, that someday it would stop. Many of us hold this same presumption: *God and I can work alone on my stuff. I can keep this private. There is no need for disclosure to anyone else.* Hiding is a really dangerous plan. Masks never work. That's like calling up the gangsters (remember those "bad guys" from the beginning of this chapter?) and inviting them right into your house for a party. Unresolved sin leads to hiding, which makes us vulnerable to even more sinning.

Ultimately, the behavior that kept Jeff's sin unresolved—and the behavior that devastated Joan the most—wasn't Jeff's vulnerability to sinful pleasure. It was that he had tried to hide his sin from her.

When we live or work in environments that encourage hiding, we don't feel safe. If no one ever asks who we are, how we feel, why we do what we do, it is easy to hide what is true about us. As a result, we begin to communicate primarily through our roles, not through our persons. We will do what is expected, but that is *all* we will do.

This is why in many organizations people can work alongside each other for years and never really know or even care who they are working with. Power, authority, position, and leverage become the unspoken means of dialogue. No one finds a place to take his or her infection out of darkness into the light, where it can be bleached of its power. What a waste! What a charade! What a loss!

The Exhausting Work of Hiding

Hiding drains us. When we hide, we can never rest. We live every waking moment with a nagging fear that someone or something will blow our cover. Hiding requires constant vigilance and maintenance. Our masks are made of papier-mâché, remember? Good material for fashioning a new look in a hurry, but get it wet and, badda-bing, we're looking like our Uncle Floyd after a face tuck! Things start to get distorted quickly. We can't stay out in public too long because we're in constant need of repair. We need a lot of down time. After a while, we can't even remember what the mask looked like the last time we put it on.

Gradually this tension creates dysfunction in totally unrelated areas. For example, if the drain of our hiding causes us to be irritable with our family, then our guilt increases, creating added stress and energy drain. The unresolved guilt, in turn, makes us feel ashamed. This takes its toll on our mental, spiritual, and even physical health. When this happens, often one of two things results. Either we will try to get caught so we can give up the charade, or another part of our life—one completely unrelated to our secret sin—will break down and collapse.

We believe that a major cause of burnout in Americans is not overwork, over-scheduling, or overactivity. It is bitterness. The load from all the unhealed wounds we carry eventually takes its toll. The breakdowns are real and rest alone cannot heal them. Such collapses will devastate the lives of those we influence and even retard their growth in trusting and loving God!

What About You?

We're at one of those stopping points again, aren't we? We want ask you several questions and offer you some hope. Maybe you are one of the thousands who could say, "They *are* writing about me!" Please know that we wrote this book to give you hope that you can begin a new way of living. Stay with us! If you do not have a leadership role in an organization or ministry, you still profoundly influence other people. And, you have an advantage: You will not have as great a temptation to hide.

Would you put a bookmark between these pages and set the book down? Before you do, ask yourself these questions:

- Would others who know me say I am one who tends to blame? Am I always criticizing the behaviors of others? Am I hypersensitive to people and their sins? Do I feel obliged to be their judge?

- Do I tend to lose my objectivity in a crisis? Do I become the issue in discussions or projects that place me under pressure or make me feel threatened?
- In my family, relationships, church, or work, is the penalty for disclosing what is true about me the same as getting caught? If so, how is that thwarting my character development?

Don't brush by these questions. If you are willing to face them, you could prepare yourself for a whole new way of living. And you could ignite a radical change in the way you protect and influence the lives of countless others. This stuff is that important.

In the next chapter we will continue to describe the painful effects of unresolved sin. If you are finding yourself in these pages, don't lose heart. God is having his way in you, even if it seems frightening and undoing. Imagine a life free from duplicity and hiding. Imagine not having to cover up what is true about you. Imagine receiving the gifts of grace that God has given you in order to heal the unresolved issues of your life. Imagine living a life without shame. Imagine feeling really alive again. That's where we're headed.

≡ DID YOU DISCOVER?

- When we are unable or unwilling to resolve the sin within us, we become sensitized toward our own sin, and others' sins. Suddenly, we become self-appointed judges of what is wrong with other people!

- Our newfound sensitivity to sin actually decreases our ability to solve the sin in our lives.

- Without the power of grace to deal with sin, we will ruin the spirit and violate the soul of those we claim to love and are responsible to love.

- One of the greatest gifts a parent, teacher, mentor, or spouse can give to others is objectivity about who they are.

- Unresolved sin is always buried alive.

- Hiding creates a double penalty: It prevents us from maturing, and it makes us vulnerable to even more sin.

- The degree to which we wear a mask in our key relationships is the degree to which our character development will be thwarted.

- If the penalty for disclosure is the same as getting caught, we will not disclose our failures.

- In an environment where sinning less is proof of godliness, almost everyone hides something.

- Hiding drains us.

CHAPTER FOUR

Behind the Mask, Part Two

"You can't hide behind a religious mask forever; sooner or later the mask will slip and your true face will be known."
—Jesus, *The Message*

Some of you may remember the science kits that parents purchased for their children at Christmas in the '60s and '70s. Today's science kits are tame by comparison. They contain things like salt, baking soda, a feather, and maybe some skin from a potato. But science kits used to contain chemicals and mysterious substances that, if mixed correctly, could take out an entire city block . . . or at least blow up the dog dish! One Saturday afternoon you'd mix a few chemicals with names like "chromium bauxite" and "manganese sulfuric tungsten" with some algae from the birdbath, and you'd burn a hole in your desk. The next day you'd mix the same chemicals with a few drops of ginger ale and you'd end up with a nasty looking boil on your hand.

Similar to a failed science experiment, it isn't pretty to watch the effects of unresolved sin in a person's life. The three-phase chain reaction that results from unresolved sin takes away our ability to have intimate relationships with others. It makes us feel ashamed and lonely and robs us of the joy that comes from showing our true face to the world. We can still picture a life of joy, but life isn't working like it used to. Something's wrong, but we can't figure out what.

Yet, even if we have lost joy and intimacy because of the devastation of unresolved sin, we can still experience a life full of beauty, a life that is better than ever. Before we learn how this can happen, let's continue our look at what we lose when we choose to hide or ignore our unresolved sin behind various masks.

Shame, blame, fear, denial, and *anger* are still mixing it up. They have three more toxic offerings in their product line of specific *inevitable effects:*

- I am unable to be loved or to love.
- I become vulnerable to wrong life choices.
- I attempt to control others.

I Am Unable to Be Loved or to Love

Wayne came to us after having been involved in a network of Christian communities whose authoritarian, legalistic leadership style caused people to feel fear, insecurity, anxiety, and weakness on the inside. On the outside these same individuals were forceful "evangelists" who rode into town with a swagger and mixed things up with gusto. Wayne was a bright, affable, sharp-looking guy with plenty of talent. He was conscientious, resolute, and loyal. He had high standards and expected others to measure up to them as well. Wayne could pick through any real or imagined holes in your theology with lightning speed.

When we met with Wayne, he gradually began to unearth his pain and hurt. As he spoke, his hands would literally shake from the fearful conclusion that he was not measuring up to God's (and his leaders') standards for spirituality and godliness. Never mind that Wayne studied his Bible and prayed and memorized and meditated and fasted and served and confessed and journaled and sacrificed more than anyone we knew. Wayne was a mess—a spiritually chiseled and polished mess—but nevertheless a mess.

Wayne was a Christian, but he had not learned how to receive God's love. And because Wayne didn't know love, he couldn't give it to others. All of Wayne's striving left him with multiple unresolved sin issues from his past, and consequently he obsessed with his current life, especially his ongoing cycles of progress and reversal.

Unresolved sin always causes preoccupation with our own lives. We want so badly to be mature and selfless, but our unresolved sin just keeps triggering self-centeredness.[1] We're consumed by the need to hide our stuff, the stuff we can't get right. We are driven to blame others in order to maintain our image of worth (or victim). We become self-directed, self-attentive, and self-protective. As a result, we are unable to offer love to others.

When we are preoccupied with ourselves, we don't see that our masquerade incites fear in those around us—that we are porcupines to be around. We gesture for people to come close with one hand, and with the other we signal, "Stay away." No wonder others consciously or unconsciously fear being intimate with us or entrusting themselves to us.[2]

We speak this involuntary, unspoken message to everyone we encounter: "I hope you like what you see. I am trying hard. But you don't really want to know me. I carry around this dark, hidden life. If you truly knew me, you'd reject me. Please, don't come close to me." Ultimately, our spouses, our friends, even our children can sense our inability to move toward them with love.

How pitifully tragic! Because we're afraid that others won't love us if they know what's really inside us, we hide our junk. But hiding the junk also hides who we are, which keeps us more separated from love than our revealed junk ever could! Hiding from others also prevents us from receiving *their* love.

When we choose to don a mask, we inadvertently hide our heart and our self from what we most desperately need—the love of others and God's love. *Unless we allow others to meet our needs, we cannot receive their love.* We talk more about this in chapter seven. It is enough here to let this fact break our hearts: Mask-wearers are the loneliest people on the planet.

I Become Vulnerable to Wrong Life Choices

Our friend Allison comes from a background of striving to be seen as a generous, caring, loving woman. Ten years ago the story of who she really was began to emerge.

Allison was attending a new church and desperately wanted to be accepted. She started to shower people at the church with gifts. Often these gifts included cash, to assist them in their needs. With the display of such a caring and loving spirit, she was quickly given opportunities to minister to many families.

After about three years of such apparent generosity, Allison met with the leadership of her church and disclosed to them that she had a serious problem with lying. "I'm really not the wealthy person I would like each of you to believe I am." The leaders didn't understand. Then she explained that she had been stealing from her employees. All the honor, acceptance, and favor she was receiving was being funded by her theft. She said, "I wanted to tell you, because my company found out and soon I will be arrested." In the course of the discussion, they asked, "Well, how much money are we talking about?" Quietly she replied, "$93,000." Allison's unresolved hurt from previous rejections fueled a series of wrong life choices and resulted in months in jail.

Caught in the trap of unresolved sin issues, we often begin to make a string of poor life choices, causing us even more harm.[3] Like the swindler, we try to fix our confusion and rationalize our wrong choices in a dozen different ways.

For example:

- Unresolved shame may cause us to flee our current situation simply to avoid the embarrassment of our circumstances. We may move to another location, not because of conviction or direction, but to escape pain.

- Unresolved blame may cause us to critique another unjustly and unfairly. We may vindictively put down others out of a critical spirit.
- Unresolved fear, leading to insecurity, may cause us to withhold the promotion of another or to shrink from a career for which we're well suited and prepared, but for which we don't feel worthy.
- Unresolved denial may cause us to reject the truth about our part in a torn relationship, costing us valuable friendships, opportunities, and influence.
- Unresolved anger may cause us to experience burnout and to lose focus and stability. We may end up leaving a spouse or a family who is the best thing that ever happened to us.

Just ask Beth. Beth would easily say she just loved her role on staff at her church. People loved her; the ministry was going well. But she would also now say it wasn't going as well as it was for several of her classmates from the college from which she had graduated ten years earlier. Some of them were actually leading large churches. A couple of them had already published books.

At first she would quietly ask, "Why me, Lord? Why are they doing so well, and not me?" Until recently she would never have been able to admit that she was becoming very jealous of her classmates. Her jealousy drove her to want to do something, something as obviously successful as what they were doing.

Seemingly out of the blue, she announced that she would be looking for another position in Christian ministry. She told people that she was convinced God wanted her to do this, but even her two closest mentors were somewhat taken back by her announcement.

Beth pursued a job, confident that she would be accepted for this significant change in career. She felt so confident that she decided to give her notice to her present employer and church. Fortunately Beth didn't get the job—it really wasn't suited for her. She defended her backfired strategy at first, until one of her mentors wisely challenged her motive. Sadly, Beth lost a wonderful opportunity to serve people who loved her and loved being with her. She made a poor choice because of the jealousy in her heart.

The jealousy, bitterness, self-doubt, and confusion that result from unresolved hurt or guilt cause many to pursue something that *isn't* them, at the loss of what *is* them. One mistaken life choice begets another. It's kind of like winding up your garden hose the wrong way. Each new loop gets you deeper and deeper into a tangled mess.

Unresolved sin issues can seduce us into wrong choices shaped primarily by current trends, media, religious experience, or even persuasive pop psychology. In our unresolved and unidentified sin, we're now blindly reacting to life without perspective, guidance, or wisdom. We close down to truth that could stop the raging *inevitable effects,* while we open up to seductive, self-vindicating reasoning.

I Attempt to Control Others

People living in the middle of the *inevitable effects* of unresolved sin find it impossible to submit to another, to trust another, or to allow themselves to need another person's love, because they have to be in control.

When we have been hurt or have hurt another, a deep need to be validated grows within us. We must, at all costs, hold onto our "rightness," and so we strive to control every area in our life. Control validates our "rightness" and soothes our anger. If we give up any form of control to another, we have somehow proven we must not be right and our anger will emerge. That's why the Pharisees, who were extremely controlling of others, revealed their politely hidden rage when Jesus challenged them about their systematic attempts to control Israel's religious and social life. Their anger erupted all over Jesus and would not be satisfied until they had him killed.

Not only must we remain in control of ourselves, but we must also control *others* in order to ensure that we don't get hurt again. As one of our friends put it, "I invested in a fortress, not only to hide behind, but to keep people out." We also control others to ensure that we will be seen as right, which fuels our permission to be angry. If they step out of line, our anger soon restores order. We reward and withhold approval based on how well others fit into our assessment of how they should live.

Such control is full of prejudice. Controllers have an incredible need to elevate what they believe at the expense of anything else. To continue marketing their claim of exclusive rightness, they must defame the competition. Controllers who run organizations or churches often tell their employees or constituency that other groups don't measure up, or that such groups are suspect and fall short of "real truth." Controllers keep repeating to themselves: "I'm it. I've got a corner on the market. Others may claim to understand some of what I know, but they're a cheap substitute. They can't get what they really need anywhere except here."

Controllers create a performance-driven environment through their endless demands on how people should live, behave, and conform. You know you're around a controller by the uneasy sense that the controller's acceptance of you can be broken without a moment's notice by a wrong behavior, a wrong allegiance, or a wrong opinion. Controllers create guarded, fearful, and edgy environments. This controlling dominance in a home, a marriage, a church, or a workplace will produce the very system Jesus condemned in the first century.[4] Performance-driven cultures can never promote healing. Rather, they create more wounding.

José and Marcia found this out the hard way. When we met them they both had a deep desire to honor God in their relationship with each other and with their children, but felt so beaten, broken, demeaned, and unaffirmed that nothing in their spirit gave them hope. Much of their previous experiences were in performance-driven environments that were overly critical, controlling, and condemning. José, who had served as an officer in performance-oriented churches, modeled these practices in his home and with his family. Through such practices, he deeply wounded his own wife and children (resulting in wounded relationships that have yet to be completely healed). José and Marcia say, "In such performance-driven environments people never discover who they really are." This family had known very few churches that were not controlling churches. One day a friend recommended that they visit a different church where they could experience a message that was full of grace and truth with no condemnation.

Why do people stay in churches like the one Marcia and José attended? Because they have never been taught that there is any other way to become godly. Because controlling pastors tell their congregations that submitting to their pastors is evidence of a person's godliness. And they, like many other controllers, will masterfully manipulate and shame their people into submission to get their own way.

At this point you are likely identifying a home, a church, a school, a ministry, or a business run by a controller or a group of controllers. Perhaps it's *your* family, church, ministry, or workplace. Or maybe you are admitting, "I am that controller. It's my family. It's my church. It is my ministry. It is my business."

Hear us when we emphatically state that *no control environment is spiritually healthy*. None. All control environments are in fact an evidence of unresolved sin. Are we speaking about God-given convictions? Not at all. Godly men and women have profound convictions. But when in the name of conviction we are controlling others, we can be sure that that "conviction" does not come from God. It comes from an unresolved life issue. Don't stay in an environment where those in responsible places need to control. No matter how godly they may seem, their influence is like spiritual kryptonite. It slowly drains away our joy and leaves us forgetting who we really are.

Controllers get their way because someone submits to them. Controllers play off of the despair of a person who feels helpless, out of control, unable to fix his or her life. These victims tell themselves, "All somebody has to do is to tell me how to live and then I can hold them responsible for my life." Now the deal is struck and the unspoken agreement between victim and his or her controller begins.

Have you ever been in such an environment? Then you know that no one in this kind of an environment takes off his or her mask voluntarily. The gamble of authenticity is way too high, because if the real you ever showed up, you'd be ridiculed and then sent away to fold socks until you get your act together.

Why do people feel compelled to control everything around them? Again we find the source in unresolved sin. Various *inevitable effects* have teamed up to convince the controller that he or she has been deeply wronged. Controllers must be "right." It is their highest value. Their assessment of truth becomes the standard of judgment by which everyone they influence must live.[5] What's really tragic is that these controllers probably *have* been wronged, maybe deeply. But their pursuit of being right robs them of being healed of the wrong done against them, and everyone they influence pays.

A Great Loss of Opportunity

Sadly, when these *inevitable effects* rule our lives, others must live without our direction or ability to give them hope.

Parents who haven't dealt with their own unresolved issues are not able to give direction to their teenagers at the most critical times in their lives. They simply don't have enough time, confidence, or freedom from their own shame to give guidance. As a result, high-school kids help each other grow up because their parents are so preoccupied with their own life issues. It's really hard for parents who haven't grown up to try to "grow up" their children. They can make judgments, give advice, even turn them to God and his Word, but they cannot with any confidence or conviction give their kids hope.

The parents of an easygoing young teen related to Bruce that their son displayed patterns of unexpected, uncontrollable anger. This respected couple told Bruce that their son's anger had repeatedly embarrassed them in public. As Bruce listened to their story, he found himself connecting the dots of family influence. As they began to tell their own story, it wasn't long before they recounted their own struggle to forgive those who had defrauded them in business dealings. Their initial disappointment festered into solidified resentment and bitterness. They verbally abused and ridiculed those who had wronged them. The load of hatred spilled over into their daily dealing with others.

Where did this pattern emerge? From a previous generation of parents who had packed their lives with unforgiveness, anger, and verbal abuse. Now, this son, who didn't have the perspective, experience, or objectivity to live independently from his parents, unconsciously responded to his own issues of hurt with anger and resentment. This is where his "unexplained fits of frenzied anger" came from.

When we have unresolved sin, we rob others of the opportunity to heal and mature in those same areas of our unresolved sin. One of the greatest opportunities we have as humans is to give others hope that the painful and destructive issues of life can be resolved. But if we have unresolved sin, we can never transfer the reality of that hope. We also cannot give direction or true correction to others struggling with sin when we are trapped in our own. Whew! Take a moment to contemplate the reality of that last sentence on those you influence. Makes a person want to sit out on the porch for a while with a stiff belt of ginger ale and reevaluate one's direction, doesn't it?

A Reflection Exercise

The remainder of this book focuses on how you can begin taking off your mask and start living in a way that keeps you from putting on more masks.

But it would be a mistake if you left this section without seeing how the *inevitable effects* of unresolved sin have worked their way into the fabric of your life. Perhaps you're thinking, *This information has helped me understand why some of the people in my life are the way they are, but I really can't see myself in these pages. I'm not aware that unresolved sin has caused me to feel shame, blame, fear, denial, and anger. I don't think I have kept others from loving me or that I have a need to control.*

If this is you, we have a brief exercise for you. Sit down by the computer or grab some paper and a pen.

1. Think of a time when you acted in sin or when an act of sin was committed against you. The more vivid and real, the more profound this exercise will be for you. This is for no one else to read. This is for you and God to review.

2. Describe what the sin was (the *act of sin*) and its initial impact on you (the *involuntary responses*)—either guilt or hurt.

3. Now, here is the most important part: If you haven't resolved the guilt or the hurt, describe why. What caused God's healing to get skipped, moving you from the *involuntary responses* right into the *involuntary effects* of shame, blame, fear, denial, or anger? Remember, unresolved sin causes a nagging sense in your heart that doesn't go away.

Some of you will recall *acts of sin* done against you as a child. Perhaps the offender was someone trusted, someone you were helpless against. You were too young to be able to identify, understand, or resolve what was happening to you, but the damage happened and you experienced lasting, internal effects. Now, as an adult, you must face that effect and damage, and allow for God's healing. He has not forgotten the event. He has not forgotten you. His memory is better than digital. It never forgets what you have tried to erase. And he has appointed a moment in time to redeem what seemed unredeemable. As perfectly as he planned the most incredible, tear-inspiring sunset, he has planned for your freedom. We encourage you not only to understand and identify what your offender did but how his or her *act of sin* affected you. Has it defined who you have become?

Or perhaps you recall acts of sin done against you in adulthood. You knew you were hurt, but somehow gave yourself permission to let the hurt and guilt go unresolved. What caused you to skip God's healing at the *involuntary responses* stage, moving you into the *involuntary effects* of shame, blame, fear, denial, or anger? What left you feeling resentment, bitterness, or perhaps alienated from a relationship?

Chapters seven, eight, and nine will ask you to consider God's solution for resolving what may have happened many years ago or just last month. For now, allow yourself to relive that season. As best you can remember, jot down the emotions, feelings, and attitudes that have since emerged. For your sake and for the sake of all you influence, don't give "super-spiritualized" answers that deny the pain. Tell the truth of your story. You are the only one who can tell this story with integrity.

4. Finally, what specific life patterns ensnared you as a result? In the last two chapters we gave an overview of just six of the dozens of specific life patterns and difficulties. You may see yourself in one or more of these six areas, or God may bring other behaviors or patterns to mind.

We hope that as a result of doing this exercise, you will agree with the following statements:

- My shame, blame, fear, denial, or anger did not just appear out of nowhere.
- I was designed with zero capability to help solve the issue of sin.
- I am able to take myself on a really profound and terrible journey.
- I lose my objectivity and perspective somewhere on this journey.
- I make really dumb choices and life decisions along this journey.
- I forfeit the love of those closest to me on this journey.
- I become incredibly judgmental of the sins of others during this journey.
- I grow tired and miserable and alone during this journey.

If you have allowed God to help you capture how unresolved sin and its three-phase process has affected you, if you can see your patterns of self-protection and hiddenness, then you are ready to follow the sign that leads to the beautiful city called Hope.

☰ DID YOU DISCOVER?

- The three-phase chain reaction that results from unresolved sin removes our ability to have intimate relationships with others.

- We deeply want to be mature and selfless, but our unresolved sin keeps triggering self-centeredness.

- Unresolved *shame* may cause us to move to another location, not because of conviction or direction, but to escape pain.

- Unresolved *denial* may cause us to reject the truth about our part in a torn relationship, costing us valuable friendships, opportunities, and influence.

- People living with the *inevitable effects* of unresolved sin must be in control. As a result, they find it impossible to submit to another, to trust another, or to allow themselves to need another person's love.

- Controllers create performance-driven environments through their endless demands on how people should live, behave, and conform.

- Performance-driven cultures can never promote healing. Rather, they create more wounding.

- When in the name of conviction we control others, we can be sure that "conviction" does not come from God.

- Parents who haven't dealt with their own unresolved issues are not able to give direction to their teenagers at the most critical times in their lives.

- One of the greatest opportunities we have in this life is to give others hope that the painful and destructive issues of life can be resolved.

- Our shame, blame, fear, denial, or anger comes from specific unresolved life issues.

- We were designed with zero capacity to help solve the issue of sin.

CHAPTER FIVE

To Please or to Trust?

*Two roads diverged in a wood, and I, I took the one less traveled by,
and that has made all the difference.*
—Robert Frost

Each of us makes a pivotal choice when we decide what to do with our guilt and hurt. We stand before two roads diverging in the woods, and our choice makes all the difference. We may not even remember making this decision, but we all make it many times in our journey. It's the most important ongoing decision any of us will make as Christians.

As we're walking down life's road, we arrive at a tall pole with signs pointing in two different directions. The marker leading to the left simply says *Pleasing God*. The pointer leading to the right reads *Trusting God*. It's hard to choose one over the other, because both roads have a good feel to them. So, we look for a third. But, at this intersection of life we don't see one. At the same time, we realize we can't jump back and forth between the paths. We must choose one. It will now mark the way we live.

Pleasing God and *Trusting God* represent the ultimate motives of our hearts. A motive is an inner drive or desire that causes a person to act in a certain way. A motive produces values that, in turn, produce multiple actions: *Motive → Values → Actions.*

Pleasing God and *Trusting God* both sound like admirable motives, and we may resent being asked to choose between the two. At this point we aren't clear why these two motives are set in contrast on this road, or if either is truly attainable. But, we are told, there can only be one motive. So we ask ourselves, "Which of these two motives best reflects the basis of my relationship with God? Is it best described as an inner drive to please God or a desire to trust God?"

Finally, we choose the path marked Pleasing God. We think, *I've got it. My mind is made up. I am determined to please God. I so long for him to be happy with me. I will discipline myself to achieve this life goal.* We begin walking down the road and are comforted to see that the path of Pleasing God is well traveled. Eventually we come to a door that reflects the values that flow from our motive—our drive or determination—of Pleasing God. A value is simply a belief that a person accepts as desirable or worthy of living out. Our values describe how we believe we should act. In other words, if our motive is a determination to please God, we will value being all God wants us to be.

Sure enough, the sign on the door reads Striving to Be All God Wants Me to Be. Because we are driven to please God, this value makes sense to us. So, we open the door by turning the knob of Effort. The motive—the determination—to please God has now produced the value of striving to be what God wants us to be. As we enter this enormous room, a host with a beautiful smile greets us, "Welcome to The Room of Good Intentions."

We like the ring of this name. And, we like that others here will see us as well intentioned.

Everyone in *The Room of Good Intentions* has the value of Striving to Be All God Wants Them to Be. They are sincerely determined to be godly. This value produces actions—actions summarized by the big banner on the back wall that reads, Working on My Sin to Achieve an Intimate Relationship with God.

As we read those words, we can't help but think, *Sounds a lot like, "Be holy as your heavenly Father is holy."*[1] *Yep. I'm in the right place.* The people in this room really want to please God by working on their sin to attain an intimate relationship with him instead of a dozen other trivial pursuits.[2] This action has sincerity, perseverance, courage, diligence, full-hearted fervency, a desire to please God, a sold-out determination, the pursuit of excellence, the right intention. *Yes,* we think. *This is definitely it! This is the place I've been looking for. I'm going to make him so happy. One day soon, we will be close. I just know it.*

Yet, as the weeks and months roll by, we can't help noticing that many people in this room sound a bit cynical and look pretty tired. Indeed, many of them seem alone or in pain. Quite a few seem superficial— guarded, perhaps? A little mask-wearing, maybe?

In time, we realize that our thinking has begun shifting too. We no longer feel as comfortable or relaxed here. In fact, we have this nagging anxiety that if we don't keep behaving well—if we don't control our sin enough—we'll be on the outs with everyone in the room. And with God!

So, we start investing more effort into sinning less, and we feel better . . . for a while.

But the more time we spend in *The Room of Good Intentions*, the more disappointment we come to feel. Despite all our striving, all our efforts, we keep sinning! In fact, some days we get fixated on trying *not* to sin. We can't seem to do enough. We never get through our list of things to work on. It feels like we are making every effort to please a God who never seems pleased enough.

This is troubling. How can a path that began with such a noble motive lead us to such an unsatisfying destination? As we're searching for the answer, a friend comes up and says, "I'm going to check out that other path back at the crossroads. For the last several years, I've given this room everything I've got, and something's not working for me. Do you want to retrace our steps and head out for the *Trusting God* trail?"

I Took the Road Less Traveled By . . .

Some of us may be considering this second road for the first time in our lives. It is "the one less traveled by." We have spent decades in *The Room of Good Intentions* and it has flat worn us out. So we now stand at the fork in front of a sign reading *Trusting God*.[3] Hmmm. Sure sounds a lot less heroic than the other sign. Even a bit ethereal and vague. And it appears to give us nothing much to do other than, well . . . trust. We're used to hearing that to get what we want we have to "sell out, care more, get on fire, buck up, shape up, and tighten up." This sign doesn't seem to be saying that, but we think, *I'm only risking a little time and effort. I can head back to the* Pleasing God *path if this turns out to be a fantasy world. Still, I'm not sure I see the difference between pleasing and trusting. But these cracks in my mask are getting bigger and bigger—I don't know how long I can keep bluffing. People have got to be catching on that something's just not right with me. This road had better not be a dead end like the other, or I'm cooked. I need answers—real answers—and quick. I'm running out of time and rubber cement.*

So, we make the choice and begin walking on life's path with the motive of *Trusting God*. At first it seems too good to be true; the path is definitely less worn than the other one. We have second thoughts every fifty yards or so. But we can no longer ignore the frustration and emptiness of the alternative, so we walk on, looking for that second door. Eventually, we spot it and as we approach we read these words written above it: *Living Out of Who God Says I Am.* We think, *This can't be right. When do I get to do something here? Where are my guidelines? But then, how big can the risk be? I can always go back if this turns out to be a ruse.* We shake our heads and, with trepidation, stoop down to turn the doorknob marked *Humility.* We step inside and immediately a host with a big smile approaches us, just like last time. This host tells us, "Welcome to *The Room of Grace.*"

As we walk into the room, we notice that it also has a huge banner on the back wall. This one reads: *Standing with God, with My Sin in Front of Us, Working on It Together.*

As we read the banner we think, *Now I'm in familiar territory. Finally,*

I get to work on my sin. But I'm not sure about this banner—it almost sounds presumptuous. I mean, imagining God with his arm around me, as we view my sin together? Is that valid? I've always believed that my sin was a barrier between God and me. If it's true that God stands with me, that changes everything.[4] I'm going to ask the people in here if they really believe that God never moves away from them, no matter what they have done. And, I'm going to find out if he is really solving their problems with them.

Despite our doubts we can't help but notice that in this room, *The Room of Grace*, everyone seems vitally alive. The people here are obviously imperfect, but they're authentic enough to figure that out. There's also a level of integrity, maturity, love, laughter, freedom, and zest that we don't recall seeing in the people in the other room. *Well, my guess is that we're not in Kansas anymore.*

Where It All Begins

Let's review momentarily. Our motives always direct what we *value* and how we *act*. For example, if we're motivated by money, we will value lucrative careers and people who can help us make money. That value will then shape how we act. It will teach us to pursue certain education, experience, and jobs. We get the word *motion* from motive; motives ultimately determine our actions. God designed us this way.

Motive → Values → Actions

This timeless sequence is at the very heart of the story of the two roads and the two rooms. Our motive as followers of Christ will either keep us in unresolved sin and immaturity or free us into God's astonishing life for us. The key to our maturity lies in our dominant inner desire — our governing motive — in our relationship with God. It all starts with motive.

To Trust Him Is to Please Him

Hebrews 11 declares, "And without faith it is impossible to please God."[5] Did you recognize the two paths in this verse? Did you notice that trusting God pleases God? If we want to please God, we must first trust him with *us*. And therein lies the problem. We were almost fine with trusting him for the Red Sea deal and the day the sun stood still, but this? Trusting him with me! Yikes, that's asking a lot more than we were bargaining for back in the first room. We'd rather work like a dog to keep him almost happy than this absurd thought of trying to trust him with me. Way too much control given away. Way too much vulnerability. Way too dangerous. Nope, not during my watch. "Waiter. Check, please!"

We all want to please God, but *pleasing* is actually a by-product of *trusting*. We arrive at *The Room of Good Intentions* out of a determination or inner drive to please God. But in that room, we discover we never can do enough to please him; we strive in vain. Worse, we learn to trust our own efforts, leaning on our own understanding, and so we never learn to live trusting God — *which alone can please God!*[6] Conversely, we arrive at *The Room of Grace* because our life motive is trusting God. In this room we learn to trust him more and discover we have pleased him wonderfully as well! The difference could not be greater.

The Deadly Trap

> If my life *motive* is an unwavering determination to *Please God,*
>> Then my *value* will be striving to be all God wants me to be,
>>> And my *action* will be working on my sin to achieve
>>> an intimate relationship with God.

When we embrace this progression and live in *The Room of Good Intentions,* we reduce godliness to this formula:

More right behavior + Less wrong behavior = Godliness

This theology comes with a significant problem: It sets us up to fail and to live in hiddenness. It disregards the godliness—righteousness—that God has already placed in us, at infinite cost.[7] This trap will sabotage our journey. Once we choose the path of *Pleasing God,* the bondage of performance persistently badgers us. Our determination to please God traps us in a formula that affixes our masks so tightly that we'll need jackhammers to get them off!

We can never resolve our sin by working on it. Oh, we may change behaviors for a while, but when we strive to sin less, we don't sin less. We actually invite blame, shame, denial, fear, and anger to become our constant companions. This formula creates the permission system for dozens of disguises. It triggers and complicates the process of unresolved sin, which causes us to lose hope. It keeps us immature! This theology is breaking our hearts. Yet, even though such harmful thinking has let us down a thousand times, we keep trying to control our bad habits and sin.

The apostle Paul tries to help us think our way out of this trap:

> Have some of you noticed that we are not yet perfect? (No great surprise, right?) And are you ready to make the accusation that since people like me, who go through Christ in order to get things right with God, aren't perfectly virtuous, Christ must therefore be an accessory to sin? The accusation is frivolous. If I was "trying to be good," I would be rebuilding the same old barn that I tore down. I would be acting as a charlatan.[8]

Many believers have spent their entire lives serving God, yet they are broken, defeated, and full of lonely despair. They have embraced a practical theology of "rebuilding their old barns"; they have placed all their efforts in "trying to be good."

The first son of Adam and Eve, Cain, chose the path of *Pleasing God* and paid dearly for it. God wanted Cain to acknowledge God's place in his life and trust God with his intentions. But Cain figured he could make God happy, and God would make good things happen for him. So Cain worked out a solution on his own terms. He brought as his offering the things that represented his *best efforts*—the fruit from his fields. Cain was "trying to be good" on his terms. When his offering didn't please God, Cain felt dishonored. Cain felt the *involuntary response* of guilt for having offered the wrong sacrifice. It didn't take long for the *inevitable effects* to follow this guilt. Cain became so filled with shame, blame, and anger that he ended up killing his younger brother, Abel.[9]

Early in his reign, King Saul likely struggled with trusting God, just like the Galatians whom Paul corrected. As a result, Saul's greatest motive was to please God. Saul thought his sacrifice would make his Creator happy and convince him to give Saul success against Israel's enemies. But God said, "To obey is better than sacrifice." He knew Saul's obedience would be the evidence of his trust.[10]

Pleasing God is an incredibly good longing. It always will be. *It just can't be our primary motivation,* or it will imprison our hearts. For if all we bring to God is our moral striving to please him by solving our sin, we are back at the same insufficient square one that put us in need of a savior. And we are stuck with our talents, skill, desire, ability, longing, chutzpah, diligence, and resolve to make it happen. Now, we've got habañera sauce on our cornflakes.

An Identity Too Valuable to Forfeit

God paid an infinite price to buy us back, to redeem us, and to give us a *new identity.*[11] So, he gets deeply disappointed when we choose not to believe what he says is now true about us. Make sense? He values our high-priced identity. He wants us to do the same. How should we show that we value it? By trusting what he says is true about us.

That's why we need to understand this progression:

If my *motive* is *Trusting God,*

Then my *value* will be living out of who God says I am,

And my *action* will be standing with God, with my sin
in front of us, working on it together.

We have explored the motive of *Trusting God*; now let's look at the *value* that flows from it—*Living Out of Who God Says I Am*. Have we already been changed? Yes. As day is from night, we have changed. We have received a new heart, for crying out loud! We have a brand-new core identity. We have already been changed, and now we get to mature into who we already are.[12]

Nature provides many examples of this incredible discrepancy between who we appear to be and who we truly are. Consider the caterpillar. If we brought a caterpillar to a biologist and asked him to analyze it and describe its DNA, he would tell us, "I know this looks like a caterpillar to you, but scientifically, in every testable result, including DNA, this is fully and completely a butterfly." Wow! God has wired into a creature that looks nothing like a butterfly, a perfectly complete butterfly "identity." And because the caterpillar is a butterfly in essence, it will one day display the behavior and attributes of a butterfly. The caterpillar matures into what is already true about it. In the meantime, berating the caterpillar for not being more like a butterfly is not only futile, it might actually harm its hearing!

So it is with us. God has given us the DNA of godliness. We are saints. Righteous. Nothing we do will make us more godly or saintly than we already are. Nothing we do will alter this reality. God knows our DNA. He knows that we are "Christ in me." And now he is asking us to join him in what he knows is true!

Paul asked the Galatian community if they could remember who *created godliness*, who made this new identity:

> Can't you see the central issue in all this? It is not what you and I do—submit to circumcision, reject circumcision. It is what *God* is doing, and *he* is creating something totally new, a free life![13] (emphasis added)

Many of us would answer Paul's question by saying, "No, I *can't* see the central issue in all this." We actually *do* think that we can strive to be godly, and it will work. We actually *do* think what we do can "create something totally new." We think we're a match for sin and the specific effects of unresolved sin—that we can control these behaviors! All we need to do is work a little harder . . . do a little more. We value striving, because we trust our own assessment of who we are instead of God's.

The Great Disconnect

Of course, many people talk as if they have taken the *Trusting God* road, but they live in *The Room of Good Intentions*. Why do so many people say the right thing, but then live the wrong life? We call this sweeping reality in the church today The Great Disconnect.

The three stories that follow come from among hundreds in our experience. We've intentionally selected three from among those who are employed in Christian work, because we believe if we can see the disconnect between talking and living *at this level,* we can easily conclude that this chasm exists everywhere in the body of Christ.

Story one. At a training forum a young woman walked up to us in tears and said, "I am very frightened and I don't know what to do, but I have to tell somebody. I am so embarrassed. We are missionaries, with three children, and for over two years, my husband, who is a teacher and executive in our mission, has engaged in major deceit and fraud. He said he wouldn't tell you, but I have to. I cannot live like this any longer."

Question: How do people who move their family to a foreign country to serve God and who rise to leadership positions in their mission and teach truth in scores of situations live in such duplicity? How can what this man believes and teaches others have so little to do with what he actually believes about himself?

Story two. Matthew is a professional counselor. He feels unloved, under-appreciated, and lonely. He has been fighting depression for more than five years. He is getting very tired and is losing the strength to keep performing. But his mask has not worn out to the point where lying is beneath him. Recently he told his organization that he was going on vacation, but the truth was that he was checking himself into a rehab clinic in order to get treatment.

Question: How can such a competently trained Christian counselor deceive others about his severe need for professional care, while attempting to offer others similar care?

Story three. Doug and Wanda presented a very impressive image of their relationship. They were marriage and family retreat speakers, and he taught future pastors marriage and family courses in a seminary. Yet Doug told us, "I am deeply angry with my wife. I have been for a long time. But my anger is no match for her long-standing disappointment in who I am and have become. She withdraws from me. Our physical relationship is almost nonexistent. We continually speak to scores of couples and families, but we are bluffing about our own marriage."

Question: How can a man and woman with such key responsibilities for transferring truth to others know next to nothing about applying that truth to their own marriage and family? At what scale of risk does the next generation find itself when being influenced by these kinds of leaders?

Jesus warns us about this very thing: "Be wary of false preachers who smile a lot, dripping with practiced sincerity. . . . Don't be impressed with charisma; look for character. Who preachers *are* is the main thing, not what they say."[14] Erwin McManus catches this fundamental issue when he says, "What I said on Sunday wasn't nearly as important as what I did."[15]

A missionary executive couple, a seasoned counselor, and professional teachers and retreat speakers. Each projected a marriage, a life, and a ministry that was "together," healthy. Each can quote Scripture on demand, teach excellent Bible lessons, and instruct others about what it means to be "in Christ." Together they influence thousands who look to them for spiritual direction. Yet, their masked reality tells a very different story about *what they really believe about themselves and their circumstances.*

This Great Disconnect pervades the Christian community. Many, many Christians never understand or live out what it means to be "in Christ Jesus." The *Pleasing God* path produces this disconnect in spades.

These stories demonstrate that our well-crafted, religiously correct words are the *least reliable* clues about our true motives. If we want to determine our real motives, our values and actions will flush them out. Look to the rooms—*Good Intentions* or *Grace*—because that's where the *action* takes place.

In other words, if I:

- Value together-looking, sanitized appearances,
- Value neatly packaged people and can't stand imperfection,
- Act to control my children in public so they'll make me look mature and put together, or
- Act out a pristine life of Christian refinement and respectable service, while camouflaging my unresolved sin under the guise of those same behaviors,

then I'm *motivated* by trying to please God . . . and I need everyone else to know that I please God. For me to hold onto my piece of the island I must maintain *at least* the appearance of living this God life. It is a motivation that everything else must serve.

Check Your Values at the Door

One more reliable way to determine our values is to listen to the *internal conversations* we have inside our head as we approach each door—*Striving* or *Living*. These inner conversations will generally line up right outside the door to either room, freighted with questions like those below. Our inner answers to the questions expose our values and will tell us which doorknob we turn and which room we enter. For example, how do you generally answer these questions?

- May I dare risk that God actually means I am a new creature right now?

- May I dare believe that God is crazy about me—right now?

- May I dare believe that God never, ever leaves my side—no matter how bad I get?

- May I dare believe that I am not on God's "B" team?

- May I dare believe that I don't have to do penance after I fail?

- May I dare believe that I don't have to put on appearances because God knows exactly the pace of my maturity?

- May I dare believe that I am considered righteous—right now—even though I still act out in wrong ways?

- May I dare believe that I am godly because I share this new nature fused with the God of the universe?

- May I dare believe that God doesn't keep a logbook of my offenses—bringing them up to me from time to time?

- May I dare believe that God never is disgusted with me?
- May I dare believe that God is never ashamed of me? *May I?*

If you answer mostly "no" to these questions, you value *Striving to Be All God Wants You to Be.* If you answer mostly "yes" to these questions, you can be assured that you value *Living Out of Who God Says You Are.* Well boy-howdy, wouldn't the latter mindset change things immensely in the day-to-day world where you receive your mail?

Changing or Maturing?

In *The Room of Good Intentions* we strive to change into something we are not yet: godly. In *The Room of Grace* we grow up and mature into something that is *already true* about us: godly. The first room creates a works-based, performance-driven relationship with God and puts the emphasis on *the effort of the one striving.* The second room places the responsibility on *the resources of God.*

God is not interested in changing the Christian. He already has. The new DNA is set. God wants *us to believe* that he has already changed us so he can get on with the process of maturing us into who he has already made us. *Trust* opens the way for this process—for God to bring us to maturity. If we do not trust, we don't mature, because our focus is messed up: *We're* still trying to change, to become godly.

Do you sense the magnitude of this distinction in resolving sin, maturing, and influencing others? This profound Scripture clearly illustrates the foolishness of striving to accomplish a change that has *already* taken place and that *only* God could accomplish in the first place:

> Does the God who lavishly provides you with his own presence, his Holy Spirit, working things in your lives you could never do for yourselves, does he do these things because of your strenuous moral striving *or* because you trust him to do them in you?[16]

If you are living in *The Room of Grace,* you aren't making desperate attempts to improve yourself. You know you cannot *change yourself;* you can only *mature* because of who you already are: a spiritually new creation born of the Spirit, a saint maturing into the image of Christ.

Those inside *The Room of Grace* place their effort just where God can use it. Ponder the contrast of how effort works in the two rooms. On the road of *Pleasing God,* effort gets me *into The Room of Good Intentions.* On the road of *Trusting God,* effort is found *inside The Room of Grace.* Effort is never a means of pleasing God or getting God's grace or changing myself. Effort is a response that God uses to work together with me on my sin, to mature into that person with whom he is already pleased. Effort born out of striving to please him never ceases to tire us. Effort born out of resting in his pleasure never ceases to renew us.

Pleasing God with the Right Motive

Pleasing God is a wonderful desire, but it never gives entry to *The Room of Grace.* Now, inside *The Room of Grace,* we can honor our yearning to please God.

When we reverse trusting and pleasing, it's like switching "trust and obey" to "obey and trust." Placing obedience before trust locks us into a mindset of obeying to please God, to earn his favor, his pleasure.

If we do not *start* with trusting who God says we are, we will end up trusting in our own resources to try to please God. This kind of self-sufficient mindset nauseates God.[17]

The following statements do not gain us entry into *The Room of Grace;* they describe the privilege and fulfillment of living in it.

- "Live a life worthy of the Lord [that you] may please him in every way."[18]
- "Offer your bodies as living sacrifices, holy and pleasing to God."[19]
- "The gifts you sent . . . are an acceptable sacrifice, pleasing to God."[20]
- "Live in order to please God, as in fact you are living"[21]

Now, we have pleasing in its proper place. The citizens in *The Room of Grace* get the privilege of experiencing the pleasure of God, because they have pleased God by trusting him.

The Goal of Life

John still remembers sitting down with Bill more than eighteen years ago when Bill was his boss. John was a young, gifted preacher, complete with four years of seminary, a snappy briefcase, and a bookshelf full of impressive-looking, scholarly books. He told Bill, "I think there are about two or three issues that I haven't yet overcome. They're not too complex or difficult. Once they get solved I really think I can be used by God in a big way."

John expected Bill to respond, "Well, let's get to work on those. What are they? Let's look at them one at a time and solve this thing so you can really take off." Instead Bill looked at John for a long time and then slowly said the words to John that God has used to change the entire focus of how he lives the Christian life. "John, then I hope that you never, ever completely solve those issues. You will become self-dependent. You will become self-sufficient. The goal is not for you to get all of your 'stuff' solved. You never will. There is an endless list of stuff. God is gracious to reveal only a snippet at a time. The *goal* is to learn to depend on—to trust—what God says is true about you, so that together you can begin dealing with that stuff."

John was headed straight for *The Room of Good Intentions* where The Great Disconnect spreads like a viral bug. You know enough about John by now to realize that the "two or three issues" remark was probably a slight understatement. Worse, the *Pleasing God* path John intended to travel would have produced two or three hundred more unresolved sin issues. But John learned about a road less traveled by. And that has made all the difference.

If you have been searching for the hope described in this chapter, come with us further into *The Room of Grace*. Discover how God's power to handle sin in this environment of grace not only resolves sin, but also allows God to do in us far beyond what we could even ask or imagine.[22]

≡ DID YOU DISCOVER?

- *Pleasing God* and *Trusting God* represent the ultimate motives of our hearts.

- If my life *motive* is an unwavering determination to *Please God*
  > Then my *value* will be *striving to be all God wants me to be*
  >> And my *action* will be *working on my sin to achieve an intimate relationship with God.*

- When we strive to sin less, we don't sin less.

- *Pleasing God* is an incredibly good longing. It always will be. *It just can't be our primary motivation,* or it will imprison our hearts.

- If my *motive* is *Trusting God*
  > Then my *value* will be *living out of who God says I am*
  >> And my *action* will be *standing with God, with my sin in front of us, working on it together.*

- Many people say they have taken the path of *Trusting God* but have ended up in *The Room of Good Intentions*. This is called The Great Disconnect.

- God is not interested in changing the Christian. He already has.

- *Trust* opens the way for God to bring us to maturity. If we do not trust, we do not mature.

- If we do not *start* with trusting who God says we are, we will end up with trusting in our own resources to try to please God.

- Citizens in *The Room of Grace* experience the pleasure of God, because they have pleased him by trusting him.

CHAPTER SIX

Grace Works!

The interpretation of grace as having only to do with guilt is utterly false to biblical teaching and renders spiritual life in Christ unintelligible.
—Dallas Willard

Every week we work with Mark, a gifted analyst and a high-capacity problem solver. As a teen, Mark became an Eagle Scout. Later he received an MBA and managed people and projects in the technology sector. Mark trusted Christ when he was a sophomore in college. From that time on, all he wanted to do was please God, to "sell out" for God, to study the Bible, to serve God anywhere in the world. Most of all, Mark wanted to get rid of the sin issues that plagued him.

In time, Mark left the business world to serve in a mission organization. We asked him to describe his life on the path of *Pleasing God* and his life on the path of *Trusting God.*

> When I came to Christ as an adult, I was desperate to turn my
> life around. I did anything and everything I was told to do to
> get rid of my sin issues—forgive, repent, memorize, meditate,

pray, serve, fellowship, disciple, commit, commit again. But, my sin issues remained and even compounded. Before I knew Jesus, relationship after relationship had discounted me. I was the son that even his own mother didn't love. She disowned me. I believed that no matter how hard I tried, I would still be worthless—and I continued to believe this as a Christian. My own sin and the sin of others against me prevented me from even *understanding* what it really meant that I had a new identity—but I was sure trying to get one.

In my fervor, I could trust God for cities, countries, nations, for thousands to accept Christ, but I could not trust God with me. I did not see myself as godly; I saw myself as valiantly trying to *become* godly. I was ready for martyrdom, to live among any tribe, but I could not live with who I was. I was a failure, doing my best to break out of my junk and hiddenness.

Over time, the effects of past sins became worse than the actual sins against me. I had become an angry, bitter man, ashamed of who I was. This mindset adversely pervaded every relationship. Simultaneously, I wanted to please God, so I was daily striving to do 110 percent for him, serving him like crazy, and getting kudos from others for doing so. I was a mess.

Then my wife and I met up with some people who actually valued others with issues—issues like mine. This was a place where people were safe to share their struggles, their painful pasts, and their present issues. This was a community of grace, where the truth of my identity would eventually become fog-free for me. I would actually begin to believe who God says I am. They actually believed I was, by God's grace, a saint. Me, a saint! They believed I had a new identity, just like theirs. This enabled me once again to get in touch with the same gift of trust God gave me when I came to know Jesus. I would begin to trust God and others with me. During those years I began to experience what I call "Spiritual Teflon." The untruths, sin issues, and the striving gradually started sliding off of me. The truth started sticking as I learned to trust.

I am a very different man, husband, father, and colleague than I was eight years ago. I am living out of who I am in Christ, not who others have declared me to be in times past. I am loving more and sinning less. I am influencing people's lives in ways that previously I could not even imagine. I am living an exhilarating life—I am living the Father's dreams for me, his very well-loved child. Trusting God's view of me has been the most intense, most difficult, and most comprehensive maturing and releasing process I have ever experienced.

Thousands have experienced the trauma and sadness reflected in the first part of Mark's story and they long to experience the second half. And they can! Explore *The Room of Grace* with us to see *how* grace works.

How Does Grace Work?

How does grace resolve our sin issues? These five truths of grace give us lasting answers for this question:

1. Humility attracts grace.
2. Grace changes our life focus.
3. Grace lets God handle sin.
4. Grace melts masks.
5. Grace changes how we treat each other and our sin issues.

Attracting God's Grace through Humility

Trust, humility, and grace guide us into an astonishing life. The road marked Trusting God leads us to a door, and when we turn the knob of Humility, we walk right into The Room of Grace. Like mutual friends introducing us to our spouse, trust and humility escort us to grace.

Humility requires trust. Humility believes that what God and others have to teach me is worthy of my dependent trust. In this case, I am depending on God to tell me how the world looks and works, giving up my rights to notions I had before. I am "leaning into" his evaluation of reality, one I did not previously have or know. This is why we define humility as *trusting God and others with me*.

Recall that God resists the proud, but he gives grace to the humble.[1] So, if a relationship or community lacks grace, that relationship or community is low on trust. One simply cannot nurture a realm of grace without trust. I can enter *The Room of Grace* only when I humbly acknowledge that I need to trust God and others with myself and give up my striving to be godly.

In 1 Peter 5 and elsewhere in Scripture we learn that grace can never be *earned*, but it can be *spurned* through untrust—the absence of humility. We never deserve grace—it is always unmerited—but we can invite grace into our lives . . . we can attract it. How? By trusting God. God gives his grace to those who trust him—to the humble.[2]

We sometimes fool ourselves by thinking we are being humble when we see ourselves in all our failure and repugnancy. We think God is pleased with our self-belittling: "O God, I am lower than sludge clinging to a rock in the deepest part of the sea, which receiving no light, causes all near to wonder if it exists at all. I am and shall remain the pitiful chorus of a hollow dirge, fit only for the recounting of what might have been."

Many people in *The Room of Good Intentions* think it is somehow pious to present themselves to God in this way. It is their way of proving that they are not proud. But their inaccurate self-deprecation proves just the opposite.

Indeed, in God's eyes this behavior exhibits not humility, but pride. Why? Because we are trusting our own assessment of ourselves and taking credit for our relative goodness. We are denying God's longing to be our goodness, our power, our ability, our strength, our healing, and our truth. That's why grace is in such short supply in *The Room of Good Intentions*. Pride shuts grace down. In contrast, humility allows us to boldly trust how God sees us and ushers us into this amazing room that specializes in resolving our sin, maturing us, and freeing us into God's destiny for us.

Back to our question: How does God in the realm of grace actually resolve my sin issues? The environment of grace provides me with truth, acceptance, healing, safety, perspective, freedom,[3] and power that I did not before know; these realities are foundational to resolving my sin issues. Conversely, prideful striving in *The Room of Good Intentions* sucks grace—and therefore power—right out of the room. That's the huge difference in the rooms. Our friend Mark did not know God's power until he gave up on his own power—which was no power at all.[4]

This shift revealed God's grace to Mark, which led him to the second insight: A healthy response to the question, "Who am I?" is "I am a person *already* deeply pleasing to God."

Grace Changes Our Life Focus

When we became Christians, something happened that *actually* changed who we are. Most of us would say, "Yeah, that's true. I believe that." If so, then why do so many of us slog on through life with unresolved sin issues? "Well, um, I guess, well, um . . . well, I'm not sure I know."

Consider this diagram. In this life, we who have trusted Christ will always have sin issues, and we will always have the identity God gave us. They are constants. Unchanging realities.

Experiencing Sin Issues ⟶

Trusting Who God Says I Am ⟶

It's key that we ask ourselves: Which one of these two constants defines my life focus? Which one do I value? If we opt for the top line, we will never experience the bottom line. But, if we focus on the bottom line, we will experience unparalleled transformation regarding our sin issues. It's a whole new way of seeing, not unlike those pictures popular a few years ago. At first glance you just saw patterns. But if you squinted and looked more intensely, you eventually saw shapes in three dimensions, revealing a beautiful and astounding picture. The first time you broke through to see such images was truly a remarkable moment. It is the same with seeing all the way through the patterns of our sin issues into the beautiful and astounding reality of who he says we are. Suddenly life is in three dimensions—alive, rich, and full of hope.

Do you see why the path of *Trusting God* is so important? We will never know our identity in Christ—and we will never live out of our identity—*unless* we start on the path of *Trusting God*. To resolve our sin issues we must begin *trusting who God says we are*. If our life focus is the top line, if we strive to eradicate our sin issues so we can somehow create a "new me" or "change me," we will always keep "me" bound to "my sin" and we will remain immature. *Trusting who God says I am* lays the foundation for maturity.

Many of us say we believe that salvation brings a "new birth," a new identity, but the way we view ourselves betrays our words; we don't believe its reality in us for a second. Instead we think, *I must keep desperately striving to become someone who will be better.* And all along we deny the mind-boggling truth that I have already become that someone.[5] In the last chapter, we called this gap between who we say we are and who we actually believe we are The Great Disconnect. It is the reason why the three of us teach that, "How I view myself is the most revealing commentary of my theology."

- It tells me about my relationship with God.
- It tells me about my relationship with others.
- It tells me whether my trust is in myself or in God.
- It tells me if I am maturing into Christ's likeness.

Letting God Handle My Sin

Many Christians know God loves us and wants to be with us, but we also believe our sin has put an impossible mass between God and us. We understand that Jesus has made a way for us to one day be together in heaven, but right now—until we get better, do better, or start to take things seriously—we believe we'll have to settle for rare moments of intimacy with him. We know ourselves too well, and there is no way we're ever going to be able to keep from sinning. We believe God loves us, but we also believe he's pretty disappointed with us. We expect to see him someday, but for now we can only hope that some days we will feel his touch on our lives. That's as good as it gets on this earth . . . or so we've come to believe.

Here's another way of putting it. Imagine a lake, maybe one hundred yards across and so wide you can't see a way around in either direction. On the other side stands someone you long to see. But you can't walk around the lake because bushes bristling with thorns and needles cover its banks. To complicate things even further, the lake water is so polluted and full of poisonous snakes and amphibious eels that it's not safe to wade in, let alone swim. You have no boat and none is in sight. What do you do? You yell back and forth across the lake in a deeply unsatisfying relationship.

The lake represents your sin, and the person on the other side of the lake is God, whom you want to be close to more than anything else in the world. Question: How do you get to him? Answer: You don't. Not unless you can find some way to remove the sin from your life. But you've got a small problem—you are pouring more sin into the lake every day.

Thousands of people heard an illustration something like this just before they asked Jesus to save them. It's an accurate picture of someone who doesn't have life in Christ, but the illustration makes no sense for the Christian. So why do thousands of Christians, now possessing the righteousness of God, live as if this illustration *still* depicts their relationship with God? They feel distant from God, imagining that a pile of sin separates them. It's as if their salvation never took place.

Ironically, striving to achieve this relationship with the Father will keep us in unresolved sin and immaturity. It produces just the opposite of what we're working for! People in *The Room of Good Intentions* hold this view. There, piles of sin separate each person from God, who is on the other side of the pile. Supposedly, moral striving will save the day, so everyone in the room keeps trying to chip away at that mound, all the while realizing they're creating a bigger pile. Then, every time they manage to change a behavior or not succumb to a poor choice, they think they have accomplished something big. This process breeds pride, not humility; sin, not maturity.

Sin will not be managed. Behavior change and sin management are deceptively tricky boxing opponents. We win some early rounds. This increases our confidence and by the fifth or sixth round, we break into a rendition of the Ali Shuffle. *Hey, this isn't so hard.* Soon, we're mugging for the cameras . . . and the next thing we know, we're on the canvas, knocked into another world by a devastating left hook.

Our efforts will not make us godly. Such thinking winks at sin. Moral striving to become godly only keeps us slaves to sin.[6] Our friend Mark lived under this enslavement . . . until he chose to let God handle his sin. He was like thousands of Christians whose life motive prevents them from living out of their new identity, who think, *If I just add this to that and that to the other thing, and keep all the dishes spinning, I'll get there!* Do you see the futility of this thinking? If the only thing we received by Christ's atoning death was a "get out of hell" card, then we have no hope of living a life worth living. Our life is as bleak as it was before we ever came to know him.

Grace teaches us to trust that God *can* handle our sin, and *only* God. Our thoughts begin to run like this: *I can't handle my sin. I can't save myself. I can't change myself. Thank you, God, for already making me godly, so you could stand with me, ready to address my sin out there in front of us. Lord, thank you there is no pile of sin and junk between us. If there were, I wouldn't stand a chance of intimacy with you. I know I can't survive away from you.*

Once, I thought that this particular sin would fulfill and satisfy me. But, Father, as we look at it together, I am learning to trust your assessment of what will satisfy me. So, what do you want us to do about this sin? I am not going to try to manage it or throw it to the ground. I trust you for the next step.

This heart-set changes our entire approach to sin. It helps us take ourselves less seriously, while taking our sin far more seriously. Now when we mess up, we can say, "Lord, this sin doesn't surprise me a bit. I hate that I am prone to sin. I am practiced. I expect that kind of thinking to trip me up at times. As a matter of fact, I can't even handle that sin, and on my own I can't even stop that sin. That's how powerful I believe sin is. I need you now."

Do you really think God would make it so hard to live a life that pleases him? What if we didn't have to work so hard? What if our sin doesn't affect how close we are to God? What if God meant it when he said, "I will never leave you nor forsake you"?[7] What if God, knowing that we don't have the power to address our sin, could walk around that impossible mass and right up to us? What if he could put his arm around us and enjoy us right now—no matter how much unresolved sin we have in our life? What if we could both stand together, looking at "my" sin, not for the sake of condemnation, but to solve it together? What if we truly believed we were without condemnation?[8] What if grace was that strong?

Welcome to life in *The Room of Grace!* Amazingly, the more we depend upon Jesus and his full ability to heal the effects of our sin, the less we sin! Now, that, friend, is like eating the grande Mexican sampler and losing weight at the same time!

Grace Melts Masks

Striving leaves us dysfunctional and immature because it creates hiddenness. Masks abound in *The Room of Good Intentions.* It is the world of false appearances. Hiddenness makes us vulnerable to sin and thwarts maturity. It breeds compulsive sinning.

In contrast, an environment of grace is full of light—not darkness. Grace creates authenticity. Why is that important? Authenticity melts masks, and reveals our true face.

The community of grace begins to break the cycle of sin issues that have kept us bound. Remember, Mark said, "I began to experience what I call 'Spiritual Teflon' in this environment of grace. The untruths, sin issues, and the striving gradually started sliding off me. The truth started sticking as I learned to trust."

How can we explain an environment of grace? It's like cool water gushing from an oversized garden hose on a hot summer day. It just keeps making us laugh with delight as it knocks us over, again and again.

Many of us understand grace as a theological position. And it is delightfully that. Undeserved, unending, unearned, unwavering, grace is God's inexhaustible love and absolute acceptance of us, coupled with his unabashed delight in us. Grace brings us adoption into God's family, a new identity, a new life, new power, new capacity, and God's full protection—with absolutely no strings attached!

But grace is much more than a theological position. Equally and simultaneously, grace is an actual environment, a realm, a present-tense reality that weaves around and through every moment of even our worst day. God's gift of grace continuously and always surrounds us. When we "approach the throne of grace,"[9] we are not coming to a throne made out of grace. The triune God lives in the realm of grace. Jesus, who lived on this earth, *came* full of grace and truth.[10]

Like any environment, an environment of grace contains intangible, yet detectable, qualities. You may not be able to see them—but you sure can feel them, just as you can detect whether you are breathing the air of a pine-filled forest or a smog-filled city. What a difference grace makes!

Trusting God means trusting that such a realm exists.

You may have experienced grace as an environment in a counseling room. Many individuals who cannot detect a grace environment in their churches or organizations are referred to counselors. These counselors often provide safety, acceptance, and hope that the believer has not sensed in his or her everyday environment. If this has been your experience, then you understand how grace works in an environment, in a relationship. And, you probably experienced a life-changing season, because grace environments bring us maturity.

To enjoy this realm, God does not ask us to get our act together or to stop sinning so much. God wants only one thing from us: He wants us to become more dependent upon him. He wants us to walk on the path of *Trusting God,* where we can begin interacting with others on the journey. When someone shows grace to us, that person begins cultivating an environment that reflects God's grace. It is an authentic, unhidden place, where our masks start melting, our sin can be known—and, therefore, addressed with the power of grace. Such places liberate the soul and change people like Mark . . . and our friend Graeme:

> By my early thirties, the thorns Christ talks about in the parable of the sower—the worries and pleasures and riches of this life—had reduced my heart's desire for Christ to a dim flicker. What caused my spiritual anesthesia? I had discovered it was easy to play the fool.
>
> Without the principles of truth and grace, practiced in relationship, the only guide I had to putting my life together was to mimic a pattern or a format or a style—somebody else's program for a successful journey with God. It got me performing my way to God, and he wasn't impressed. Then I encountered some people who showed me grace. Solomon said there is nothing new under the sun, but an environment of grace was new to me. The truths about how God sees me and who I am in Christ came roaring into my life.
>
> I discovered that if these truths are trusted, they infect everything. They're the foundation for my marriage, how I deal with my kids, how I do ministry, live life, and how I work as a lawyer.
>
> Blaise Pascal sewed into his coat a piece of paper with these words on it: "Fire, God of Abraham, God of Isaac, God of Jacob, not of the philosophers and scholars. Certainty. Heart felt joy. Peace. God of Jesus Christ. Joy, joy, joy, oceans of joy." Ten years ago I would have envied him. Today, I join him.

Grace Changes How We Treat Each Other
When We Sin

When we live in *The Room of Grace*, we begin to relate to others differently. We begin to experience true intimacy. Do you know why? For the same reason we no longer have distance between God and us. Grace wonderfully reorients all our relationships.[11]

We no longer see one another with our sin between us. We no longer see one another through the grid of our shame, blame, and anger. We no longer feel we must compete with each other. We no longer come to our relationships feeling ashamed, condemned, and unacceptable. We no longer hide our real faces from each other. We begin to discover that our character is actually formed in relationships. We stand in front of each other, true-faced. Safety, protection, and love characterize the relationships in this room rather than mistrust, deceit, and guardedness.

We see one another as saints who sin, rather than as sinners who are saved. If we truly believe in our heart of hearts that we are saints, then we're able to stand with each other in the reality of our sin. But if we don't believe that, and instead view each other as sinners, we will demand that others work on their sin in order to have a relationship with us. Naturally, we will be tempted to hide our sin from one another. We cannot divorce how we view ourselves and our sin, from how we view others. If we think, *My sin is between God and me,* then we will also think, *Your sin and my sin stand between us.* And we will make the same mistake of striving to work on our sin so we can have a better, closer relationship. Not only does our sin not improve, but we feel even further from him and too tired to enjoy him even if we could! We'd almost be better off to ignore the sin and go fishing. At least we might catch a fish.

After connecting with this truth of grace for the first time, two men walked up to Bill. Ryan said, "I have known my friend Sam here for many, many years. We have a deep relationship. Over lunch we did the exercise that encourages us to choose to believe that we are each saints. During that exercise I learned something about Sam that he has kept hidden from me all this time." Ryan then turned to Sam and said, "Why don't you share with Bill what you just told me."

Sam said, "I told Ryan that once, a pretty long time ago, I acted out in unhealthy behavior, and that I am presently deeply tempted to do so again. In fact, I just wish someone would hit on me."

When Sam finished, Ryan said, "Not long ago, if you would have told me what you told me today, I would have rejected you, Sam. I would have pulled away from you. Today I cannot do that because I know you are a saint and my brother. I don't understand why all the stuff you told me is true. I feel deceived. You've lied to me for many years. I feel hurt and confused. I have a thousand questions and I don't have a clue how to help you with what you just told me. But, Sam, I can tell you that I am proud of you for telling me. And I will stand together with you, because I know who you are. You are a saint, Sam. You are a saint with some pretty deep issues that are freaking me out at this particular moment. But you are my brother. I will not walk away from you."

When our theology gives us permission to see Christians as sinners, we give ourselves permission to reject them. Ryan saw his friend for who he was—a saint. So he could literally put his arm around Sam and weep over the reality of what was true. Ryan didn't send his friend away to deal with his sin. He intentionally walked with him into God's resolution. That's what God models and teaches us to do in *The Room of Grace*.

For years, these two men had seen each other only as saved sinners. They were terrified to disclose what was true in their lives. They instinctively knew they were viewed as sinners first and would receive the condemnation of a sinner. Now the spell had been broken. Sam had disclosed a significant area of struggle in his life, and both were seeing each other as fragile and compromised, but dearly accepted saints.

When we trust God, we live by a value: *The godly are those who trust God with themselves*. Period. Sounds like Hebrews 11, doesn't it? The godly ones are those who live by faith (trust). Sounds like Romans 3, doesn't it?

Grace's permission radically changes how we see each other and how we deal with sin. We can now be exactly who we are, with all our issues and problems and unresolved stuff, and still fully experience grace, love, and acceptance. That single reality is perhaps the greatest feeling in this room. It resolves sin issues. This room has no caste system. No superstars or pretenders. Flawed and broken and fragile people are celebrated for their vulnerability and dogged dependence upon their identity in Christ.

As we begin to believe these truths, we become the kind of safe place for others that J. R. R. Tolkien describes in *The Fellowship of the Ring*. "Frodo was now safe. . . . The house was, as Bilbo had long ago reported, 'a perfect house, whether you like food or sleep or storytelling or singing, or just sitting and thinking best, or a pleasant mixture of them all.' Merely to be there was a cure for weariness, fear and sadness."[12]

The Ultimate Goal

Some of you briefly caught sight of a previously unseen streak of light flashing through *The Room of Grace*. Hope awakened. Wonder stirred in you. Yet, you struggle to describe the splendor you sensed.

The sensation we believe you felt is this: Resolving sin is only the *starting point* of life in *The Room of Grace*. God's final objective for us is not resolving sin or "getting well." God's ultimate goal is maturing us into who he says we are and releasing us into the dreams he designed for us before the world began.[13] That's where all of this is going. That's why your hope awakened. When we swim in the ocean of God's grace, we can't help but respond with playful abandon. We will grin, laugh, and splash around. We will burst into song at inappropriate times, dance, play, serve, fall on our knees in worship, give our lives away, and embrace each other. We'll sin less. We'll love more. We are free.[14] And, we'll naturally think about others. We'll sacrifice to reach to the lonely, the lost, the helpless, the forgotten. Everything, *everything* seems fresh, vibrant—alive. We find ourselves pausing in the middle of a busy day, shaking our heads and whispering, "Go figure . . . *me.*"

Astonishment fills Mark and Graeme's stories, in part, because in their maturing they began influencing others beyond what they could have imagined! God carefully designed his "influence system" so that we would have to influence far more out of *who we are* than *what we do*.[15] Therefore, God's "influence system" *requires* personal maturity. Do you see *why* God so deeply wants us to mature into the "likeness of his Son"?[16] There is no profound influence without it.

Note well this sequence of truths:

- We cannot profoundly influence others without maturing.
- We cannot mature without finding resolution to our sin issues.
- We cannot find resolution to our sin issues without trusting who God says we are.

As we live into this cluster of truths, our life diagram expands to illustrate the profound purpose of life in *The Room of Grace*. Resolving sin is not the ultimate goal of grace; maturing and destiny are the endgame— God's dreams for us.

Experiencing the Ultimate Life

Our friend Cary is living this astonishing life. He recently celebrated his fortieth birthday. His wife threw a surprise party for him and invited dozens of his closest friends. Cary came into faith with several dozen addictions, compulsions, dysfunctions, and twisted family dynamics. He's been a Christian for several decades, and yet he still struggles with the effects of all that junk. Cary is not "fixed." It's likely he will struggle with significant issues for the rest of his days on earth. But Cary is healthy and resolving sin. He believes in his identity and, as a result, is doing profound stuff for God's glory, because he came to trust God's assessment of him, even in the middle of pain.

Despite Cary's "failure" to get his whole act together, almost every person at that party stood up and spoke of the countless ways he had been used in their lives. There were many tears, long hugs, and heartfelt affirmations of how caring and important a friend he had been to each of them. The sharing must have lasted two hours! Anyone watching would have concluded that Cary is a significant minister to that community.

The following week, Cary dropped off some chairs at John's house and told him, "You know I am meeting with a counselor. I told her about the birthday party last weekend, the affirmation and all the things others said were true about me, in spite of all the junk I know is in me. And she said to me, 'You are one of the truly lucky ones. Very few have the life you have been given. I envy you.' She said she envied *me*!"

John looked long and hard into the face of this man he'd been through so much with and said, "Cary, you prove the penalties of being messed up every day, in new and exciting ways. But you have come to believe who you are in Christ. And so, you are not sick, but healthy. And there are about a hundred of us who are deeply privileged to know you, because knowing you has made us better people."

Do you see how *The Room of Grace* helps people trust who God says they are and then deal with sin in a new way that enables them to mature? Grace allows them to strip away the veneer and trust God with their sin, their healing, and their growth. They are fragile, vulnerable people who rely on God's strength in the midst of their often-compromised existence. It is breathtaking to behold.

Do you not have a *Room of Grace* where you live? Here's hope: You can begin creating such a room, even if it's just with one other person. Remember, the power is not in a ready-made room that you somehow stumble into; *the power is in the grace.* It's God's grace, and you can attract his grace all by yourself—through a humble heart. He loves to give excessive amounts of grace to humble people. Trust God and others with you, and see if this room doesn't start taking shape right before your eyes.

Getting to the Payoff

Many of us may not think much about our influence on others, because unresolved sin keeps us immature and thinking mostly about ourselves. We come to Christ "me-centered," and we struggle to progress beyond that condition. The wonderful dreams God has for us often remain unclear because unresolved sin issues block our view. In our immaturity we may even think that our dreams for ourselves are more significant than what God has planned for us.

God thinks about our influence on others *all the time.* He designed us to influence others.[17] And, every so often, we catch a glimpse of the destiny God has planned for us, and new longings stir within. We fill up with fresh motivation to learn how grace works and to follow God's voice into a land of adventure and fulfillment. Then we struggle to remember the entry point to that great land. It's like standing outside the bakery, face pressed against the window, smelling the fresh bread and pastries inside, but we can't locate the door to get inside, where we would surely sample every wonderful treat in those glass cases. Remember the door to the "bakery"? It's the door that teaches us *how to live out of who God says we are* by turning the doorknob of *humility*, opening wide into *The Room of Grace.*

We need to tell you one more thing about *how grace works,* something you can look forward to in *The Room of Grace:* You receive gifts there. Gifts for every occasion and every need. Jesus passes them out for the asking, to meet specific needs. God has three gifts created specifically to heal your wounds and resolve your sin. Gifts essential for maturing us and giving us the desires of our hearts.[18] In the next three chapters, we'll encounter God's powerful grace gifts of love, repentance, and forgiveness. We'll see how grace actually changes how we apply these truths in resolving sin and maturing the *real you.* So, here's to your true face, a face that, with increasing brilliance, reflects the majesty of our great God.[19] It might almost seem too good to be true, if it wasn't.

≡ DID YOU DISCOVER?

- These five truths of grace give us lasting answers for resolving our sin issues:
    - Humility attracts grace.
    - Grace changes my life focus.
    - Grace lets God handle sin.
    - Grace melts masks.
    - Grace changes how we treat each other and our sin issues.

- We define humility as *trusting God and others with me*. Therefore, if a community lacks grace, that community is low on trust.

- Pride shuts down grace.

- The environment of grace provides me with truth, acceptance, healing, safety, perspective, freedom, and power that I did not before know. These realities are foundational to resolving my sin issues.

- *Trusting who God says I am* lays the foundation for maturity.

- How I view myself is the most revealing commentary of my theology.

- Striving leaves us dysfunctional and immature because it creates hiddenness.

- Grace creates authenticity. Authenticity melts masks.

- Safety, protection, and love characterize relationships in *The Room of Grace*, rather than mistrust, deceit, and guardedness. We stand in front of each other, true-faced.

- We need to see one another as saints who sin, rather than as sinners who are saved.

- When our theology gives us permission to see Christians as sinners, we give ourselves permission to reject them.

- God's final objective for us is not resolving sin or "getting well." God's ultimate goal is maturing us into who he says we are and releasing us into the dreams he designed for us before the world began.

- God carefully designed his "influence system" so that we would *have to* influence far more out of *who we are* than *what we do.*

- We cannot profoundly influence others, without maturing . . .
  We cannot mature without finding resolution to our sin issues . . .
  We cannot find resolution to our sin issues without trusting who God says we are.

CHAPTER SEVEN

The Supreme Gift of Grace: Love

Grace is the face that love wears, when it meets imperfection.
—Joseph R. Cooke

You may be deeply encouraged by the last two chapters and at the same time feel somewhat depressed. You may be thinking: Why didn't I learn this stuff earlier? I now realize I missed out on that second room I should have entered long ago. Wasted years spent in *The Room of Good Intentions* affixed my mask so tightly that it is now really hard to take off. My time there gave me scars I fear I will always carry.

For you, here is really, really good news. When you enter *The Room of Grace*, Jesus has some gifts for you. Gifts for every occasion and every need. They are given for the asking, to meet your specific needs. For every issue, every unresolved sin, every wound, God has created a gift specifically to meet that need, resolve that sin, and heal that wound.

In the middle of our misery, Jesus taps us on the shoulder and says, "I have something for you that cost me everything to get for you. Here, it's a gift of my grace for you." Written across the gift is one word: *love*. The attached card reads: "Take it, apply it, and trust me to make it real. I love you. Jesus."

Love, the first gift of grace, acts as a solvent to lift our masks. It acts as a balm that can begin to heal our unresolved sin so that we never want to put on a mask again. Those who receive this gift live in profound and sacred health . . . without fail . . . always.

Degenerated Love

You may be surprised to learn that this gift of love is not about "learning to love more" or "learning to love better." In God's world, receiving love comes *before* giving love. We learn how to love only when we first learn how to receive the love of God and others. "We love because he first loved us."[1]

We so much want to *do* something. Most of us have never been taught how to let something *be* done to us. We haven't learned the fine art of *receiving love*. But because we've been urged to love others, we charge forth to inflict others with our "love."

Our friend, Don, turned love into a hurtful imitation of the real thing. He is a quick-thinking, fast-acting investment broker whose family of origin probably invented the word *dysfunction*. As we were mentoring Don on learning to receive love, he told us: "All my Christian life I was challenged to love other people. But why? Why would anyone want my version of love? That's just asking for trouble. These were *my* love gifts:

arrogance packaged as teaching; control disguised as protection; manipulation wrapped as concern; exploitation marketed as opportunities. How 'bout them love gifts! Until I learn how to *be* loved, my 'loving' just spewed all my junk and debris onto others."

A Process of Meeting Needs

The knowledge that we are loved, accompanied by three dollars, may get us a good cup of coffee—but it will never peel away our masks or heal our wounds. "Knowing about love" and "experiencing love" are not the same thing.[2] They come from two different planets . . . or two different rooms. In *The Room of Good Intentions* we will hear a lot about love, and our spirituality may even be assessed by how much we "love" (do for) others. However, in *The Room of Grace* we actually learn to *receive* the gift of love—to experience it.

When we are ready to receive love, we will know, because we will begin to *experience a process* with the following steps:

1. I understand that I have needs.
2. I realize that having my needs met is experiencing love.
3. I freely admit that I desire to be loved.
4. I choose to let you love me.
5. I let you love me—on your terms, not mine.
6. I am fulfilled when I have experienced love.
7. I am now able to love others out of my own fulfillment.

STEP ONE: I Understand That I Have Needs

In our coaching forums we occasionally ask people to get away by themselves for a while and list their *needs* for developing spiritual health and maturity. A need is something required and indispensable—a must. A number of people come back with a very short list, some with a completely blank page. Some don't come back at all. They just *need* a nap!

What causes us to overlook or avoid the basic requirements for our health and maturity—our needs? The principal reason is that we see our needs as weaknesses. Ironically, we have no problem accepting our need to breathe as imperative for our physical health. Meeting our need for security, attention, and acceptance is just as normal and necessary for our spiritual health as meeting our need for oxygen is for our physical health. Sin influences people to define their innate needs as weaknesses. "I don't need you" is the language of the wounded heart.

Our weaknesses are actually those attitudes and behaviors that emerge because of the unresolved sin in us. Our weaknesses also stem from our unwillingness to accept our limitations. For example, if I'm not athletic enough to dunk a basketball, then I lie about a knee injury.

If we see needs as weaknesses, we will hide our needs and limitations and call it self-reliance. Or we'll pretend that we have no needs and call it independence. Or we may believe no one should ever have to meet our needs and call it strength. Or we believe that as we get more "spiritual," we outgrow our needs. This, we say, is maturity.

Some of us take our aversion to needs a step beyond weaknesses—

we actually confuse our needs with sin. *That* must thrill God. *He's* the one who created needs. Needs do not come from sin, and they are not sin. Adam and Eve *needed* the love of God long before they sinned! God communicated with them and fulfilled their needs in that relationship of love. God accepted them. He gave them security. He gave them attention and boundaries for their health and safety.[3] Needs are not sin, but sin has distorted our understanding of needs. In our destructive, self-centered world, we hardly know what to do with our needs.

So, the first step in receiving the gift of love is to understand that we have needs. Once we believe that, we are ready for step two.

STEP TWO: I Realize That Having My Needs Met Is Experiencing Love

Why did God create us with needs? Most of us have never thought about this before: Without needs we cannot experience love—we cannot know when we are being loved.

Think about it. A desk has no need to be loved. We may say we "love" a certain desk, but disappointing as it may be to some, the desk will never know our love. It has no capacity for love. Needs give us the capacity to feel loved. We know or experience love when our needs are met. This is why we say that love is the process of meeting needs.

Every day we need to be loved. Every day our God is committed to meeting our needs for attention—his servant love[4]; acceptance—God's unearned love[5]; security—God's committed love[6]; trust—God's faithful love[7]; guidance—his disciplined love[8]; truth—God's instructional love[9]; protection—God's jealous love[10]; significance—God's affirming love[11]; and so forth. These needs never go away.

Sadly, if we cannot identify our needs, we cannot know love. If we deny we have needs, we will not experience love. If we withhold our needs, we can't receive the love others have for us. And, if we don't know love, we'll be stuck with open wounds that will not heal—those nasty *inevitable effects*. And, when our needs go unmet, we are truly unhappy people. Period.

STEP THREE: I Freely Admit That I Desire to Be Loved

Deep within each of us resides the desire to be loved. Oh, but the pain and risk of love! We creatively fashioned some of the oldest masks in our closet to make others think that, at least in our case, love is optional. These masks come complete with habitual mannerisms, clever responses, and insulating possessions—all ingenuously designed to convince others that we have no longing to be loved.

Into our silliness God often steps in and arranges circumstances to expose our absurd antics. He graciously turns our denial into a life-changing admission that, "Boy-howdy, how I desire to be loved!" Such a God-moment happened to Rick, one of Bill's students in a graduate class. Rick heatedly interrupted Bill's teaching to declare that he had no needs. Rick explained that now that he had his relationship with the Lord, the Word of

God, and his responsibility as a Bible teacher, all his significant needs had been met. He was adamant and became the focus of attention in that class.

The following week Rick stood up in class and asked if he could explain what had happened to him the previous week in a church class he was teaching. He then proceeded to tell the class that shortly after he began teaching, a gentleman named Joe sat down in the front row and started weeping. Rick was deeply disconcerted because there had never been much emoting during his teaching before. He kept on teaching, but Joe wept through the entire class. After the session everyone left the room, except Joe. He walked up to Rick and said, "I really need you to help me." Joe was now sobbing loudly. Rick replied, "Well, I'm not a counselor, but maybe I can listen to your problem." Joe explained that he was devastated because two days earlier his wife of more than fifteen years left him for another man and moved away overnight. Rick was deeply affected by this man's words but didn't know how to show it. He eventually gave Joe a clumsy hug, trying to care for him.

At this point, Rick slowly looked around Bill's classroom and told everyone that some years earlier his wife had also walked out on *him*. He had not told this to anyone at the school before. He had tears in his eyes. Then he looked at Bill and said, "I was wrong. I have incredible needs and I have frozen them all these years. I have lived in denial. I so wanted what you were teaching not to be true because I never wanted to be hurt again. Last week, when I stood up, I was projecting onto everyone else a denial of my pain. I was filled with resentment for what my wife had done to me. For me to admit that I had needs meant I had to risk being loved again. I know God sent Joe to remind me of the pain. I have lived in isolation from love all these years." He then wept openly and told the class, "I am unbelievably miserable and I need help."

Thousands know Rick's pain. The loss of his wife devastated him, and he thought he had figured out a way to deal with it: *I will take care of myself. I won't get that close again.* Just like so many others, he assumed his needs for intimacy, acceptance, security, affirmation, and the like would go away. But God hardwired needs into us—they don't go away.

Rick hid his pain somewhere deep within so it wouldn't embarrass him anymore. Little did he know that this choice of denying his *involuntary response* of hurt would cause him to experience the *inevitable effects* of shame, blame, fear, denial, and anger. Rick had not recognized the devastating *sequence* of unresolved sin. But you can. If God speaks to you through Rick's story, it means he may not need to send you a "man in the front row" before you freely admit that you want to be loved.

Many of us have spent years perfecting our self-protection routines. We have carefully, stone by stone, erected a drafty castle that we thought would safeguard us from the pain of broken relationships. Some of us had "good reasons" to erect that castle. But we now know that these walls have never truly protected us—they have just kept us isolated and alone. Our only companions were those nasty gangsters, the *inevitable effects* of shame, blame, fear, denial, and anger.

Our castle walls won't come down just because someone says they should. They start coming down when we admit:

- Step one, we have needs;

- Step two, we can only experience love when our needs are met; and
- Step three, we really, really want to be loved.

And, that, our friends, is when the fun begins!

STEPS FOUR & FIVE: I Choose to Let You Love Me— on Your Terms, Not Mine

After chronicling Sharon's shocking childhood in chapter two, we wrote that she'd be back to tell "the rest of the story." We tell that story here to give you hope. Rarely has any child been subjected to such ongoing treachery and evil as Sharon, and yet today all three of us consider her one of the healthiest and most mature leaders in our lives. If God can resolve her sin and the sin done against her, he can do it for you too. How did Sharon progress from such devastation to mature influence? Much of it occurred right here through steps four and five.

As an adult, Sharon invested years designing and building one of the more exquisite self-protection structures around. She says, "I built the Great Wall of China." But, behind this formidable wall, those relentless *inevitable effects* ultimately wore her out. When she could take no more, Sharon started asking questions, and a friend began walking with her down the trail of *Trusting God*. Sharon admitted her needs and that they would never be met unless she learned to receive love. In time, she began trusting who God says she is, and that ushered her right into *The Room of Grace*.

Not long after that, Sharon began realizing the central role trust would continue to play in her healing and maturity. She learned the fundamental truth behind step four: The degree to which I *let* you love me is the degree to which you *can* love me, no matter how much love you have for me. That wouldn't have been a problem for Sharon, except the "let" requires trust! We cannot *let* another person love us unless we trust the person.[12]

People who are unable to trust will *never* experience love. *Ever.* One can't find a way through that particular cul-de-sac. Despite the years of abuse, Sharon avoided that lonely life, because she learned to entrust herself to God and others. If anyone had reason never to trust again, it was Sharon. But, she *let* people love her and her needs began to be met in a profound way. Grace, when it is conceived in trust, begets astonishing resolution, healing, maturity, and powerful influence.

Many people who deeply want to be loved are not loved, because they won't turn that doorknob of *Humility* — "trusting God and others with me." They stand out in the cold, outside *The Room of Grace,* in pain (and blame) because people don't love them. But, Sharon's life demonstrates this truth: The people God wants to use to love you deeply and to meet your needs stand right on the other side of that door. Turn the knob.

There's another dimension of receiving love that Sharon's story illustrates. Step five says, "I let you love me on your terms, not mine." When Sharon was first learning to receive love, she demanded that people do this or buy that or serve her in the way she deemed best. But, as she matured in receiving love, she realized that submitting to others to meet her needs required that she let *them* discern *how* to address her needs. In learning to receive love, we cannot forget that *others* are the ones with the strengths that can meet our needs. *We* are the ones with both the needs and the inability to meet them. Learning to let others love us on their terms is part of what it means to "submit to one another out of reverence for Christ."[13]

If, despite our need for acceptance and people's moves to include us, we continually reject them because we want them to meet our needs on our terms, we will remain unloved and in the darkness of our unresolved sin. We cannot experience another's acceptance, love, or guidance unless we *let* that person give us these things.

> Lost in the darkness
> Silence surrounds you.
> Once there was morning
> Now endless night
>
> If I could reach you,
> I'd guide you and teach you
> To walk from the darkness
> Back to the Light.[14]

Will others meet our needs perfectly and will we trust perfectly? No. This is *The Room of Grace*, remember? "Grace is the face love wears, when it meets imperfection." Learning to love perfectly or trust perfectly is not the point; rather, it's learning to receive love. We can't wait for perfect people before we trust people. That's like standing in line at the DMV without a number and expecting prompt service. It ain't gonna happen!

Further, when we on the basis of trust receive God's perfect love for us, it pushes away our fear and teaches us to embrace the love that heals our wounds.[15] In *The Room of Good Intentions,* where self-protection rules, we put everything in jeopardy—our healing, our maturing, and our reason for being on this earth. But in *The Room of Grace* we have learned that God won't let us down, even when others do. When they turn away, we remember he won't.[16] He's our safety net. He's got our back. Trusting God frees us to move into these relationships. Trusting God frees our hearts to experience *his* safe, constant, intimate sufficiency. Sharon would tell you that this solid strength of trusting God—who can't let us down—allows us to move *toward* others in love despite the risk. And that propels us into a different dimension of living.

STEP SIX: I Am Fulfilled When I Have Experienced Love

Trusting God is the path that leads us into *The Room of Grace* where we gradually receive the supreme gift of grace—love. If we have spent our lives building walls of self-protection, it will take time and trust for us to unwrap this gift. But when we receive love—when we are loved— we feel fulfilled. Love completely satisfies our longings, ambitions, and potential. God, the ultimate fulfiller, invites us to trust him. Those who hang out very long in *The Room of Grace* always experience too much love to return to a life without such a gift.

What does this new way of living do to a person? For those who've never or rarely experienced it before, it is nothing short of miraculous. Others can actually see a real and lasting difference. Wives look at their husbands, shake their heads, and ask, "Who are you, and where has my husband gone?" Received love turns frightened pretenders into confident dreamers. It even turns violent lions into humble and tender receivers of love.

Maybe pain is the reason you are reading this book. You know something is wrong and don't know how to fix it. Maybe you know you are hurting others and don't know how to stop. Maybe your pain is the absence of peace. Maybe your pain is the worst type of all—the pain of hiding, isolated in a private world where love cannot penetrate.

Centuries ago, as legend has it, an escaped slave named Androcles fled into a forest where he wandered upon a loudly growling lion. Androcles started to run, but when he noticed that the lion did not pursue him, he turned around and slowly approached it. At that point the lion lifted out its paw, swollen and bleeding. Androcles immediately saw the source of the pain—a huge thorn had buried itself deep within the lion's paw. With great courage, knowing that the removal of the thorn would temporarily increase the lion's pain and possibly incite it to attack, Androcles removed the thorn and bound up the paw. When he finished, the lion licked Androcles' hand like a dog and took the young man to its cave. Every day the lion would bring meat to him.

Then, one day, both Androcles and the lion were captured. Their captors decided to withhold food from the lion for several days, and when it was good and hungry, they would throw Androcles to the lion to be eaten. When the appointed day arrived, the emperor and his court came to witness the spectacle. Androcles was led into the middle of the arena and the lion was loosed from its cage. Immediately the lion roared at its victim—but then recognized a friend. The lion stopped and leaned into Androcles, rubbed its face against the young man's, and then licked his hand again, like a dog. Shocked, the emperor summoned Androcles, who recounted the entire story. The emperor set Androcles free and returned the lion to its home in the forest.

As beautiful as this fable is, it is not even close to the beauty we can find when we allow others to love us. Andrea, our close friend, was not unlike the lion. Brilliant, well-read, shrewd, and intimidatingly competent, Andrea always made you feel like back-pedaling in her presence. John says, "I always felt if I were to make a mistake or say something uninformed in her presence, I'd be instantly and forever labeled, and then banished by her into the huddled masses of the dim-witted. I'd politely try to answer her questions, sounding more like a politician behind in the polls than myself. She was strong, sharp-tongued, blunt, and overwhelming."

We had no way of knowing that Andrea's paw had been swollen and bleeding for some time. She was simply trying to find out, in her own way, if we would answer her gruffness in kind, or if we could help pull out her thorn. We provided Andrea with an environment of acceptance, affirmation, protection, and truth, and this environment helped her feel safe. Along with others in our community, we saw Andrea as a saint—a saint with claws, to be sure, but still a saint! Yes, sometimes her claws hurt us, but that's what happens when we live in *The Room of Grace*. Grace-givers understand this. After all, Jesus, who was full of grace and truth, took all of our pain on himself so that we could be healed.[17]

For several months, Andrea's pain drove her to seek out several of us to whom she could bare her heart's pain. Her world wasn't working. Her mask-of-choice caused her to feel lonely and unloved. She could not receive the love we offered her. But this lioness had the courage to humble her heart and dared to trust some fallible and fragile people to do what she could not do for herself—meet her deep need for security, for dependency, for hope. At first, Andrea's requests for help were clumsy. After all, this was unfamiliar territory for her. But it made her story all the more lovely to those of us who knew and loved her.

Because of her humble choice to receive love, Andrea now lets others love her. It is hard to believe she is the same woman! Losing none of her competency, she has become a lover of others and a playful friend who laughs often and cries freely. We feel safe around her and have known her continual affirmation and trust.

Andrea is a powerful woman who travels in powerful circles. But if we are ever pitted against each other in the arena, we know Andrea will look into our eyes, lean into us, and rub her face against ours—no matter how great the pressure or how hungry she is in the pain of what sin has done against her. Andrea is fulfilled in love, and now she has enough for others, which leads us to the final step.

STEP SEVEN: I Am Now Able to Love Others Out of My Own Fulfillment

Having our needs met by receiving the love of God and others is not just about "feeling better"; it's about fulfillment. *To fulfill* means "to meet the requirements of, to satisfy."[18] When the requirements of our soul—our needs—are met, it satisfies us. This fulfillment produces inward peace, contentment, and healing for our wounds. As our wounds heal, we can turn away from them with a fresh passion, confidence, and love for others. To serve others out of a contented, fulfilled soul is like rubbing eucalyptus oil onto the sore muscles of a friend. The person gets healing and the whole room smells wonderful.

Millions of people have yet to meet the King of Love. When they see us living in blame, shame, fear, denial, and anger, with no real answers, it confuses them. When they see us attempting to mask those dysfunctions, it tells them not to trust us—or the God we follow. When they see us focused on wounds that never heal, they conclude we cannot deal with theirs. That's a major reason why life in *The Room of Good Intentions* is such a waste. It never produces an environment conducive to people courageously attempting their first footsteps of trusting the grace and love of Jesus Christ.

If it is unerringly true that each of us enjoys only the love we will allow in, and if it is equally true that God went to unending lengths to bring us love in a way that we would allow in, then it becomes stunningly obvious that the carriers of God's love ought to be wildly driven to learn to give his love in a way that can be easily put on.

To give a love that can be trusted changes everything. This is where life gets worth living. It jump-starts one of the most profoundly beautiful and miraculous chain-reactions we get to witness in this lifetime. Closed, broken, frightened, bluffing men and women come squinting out of the dark corners into the light and start singing songs they didn't know were in them. They begin to feel alive-secure in his embrace, seeing life for the first time in full color. Actually allowing this love past their double-bolted defenses, they wonder out loud what took them so long. Each one becomes real, safe, creative, and refreshingly untamed. They drink this love in like those gulping down cold, fresh lemonade for the first time. And they almost involuntarily begin to offer to all around them a love as rich and freeing as what they are taking in. They discover a waiting, thirsty community everywhere they look. And the world around them dramatically changes, one drink at a time . . .

≡ DID YOU DISCOVER?

- Love, the first gift of grace, acts as a solvent to lift our masks off our faces.

- Those who receive this gift live in profound and sacred health . . . without fail.

- In God's world, receiving love comes *before* giving love.

- When we are ready to receive love, we will know, because we will begin to *experience a process* with the following steps:

  - I understand that I have needs.
  - I realize that having my needs met *is* experiencing love.
  - I freely admit that I desire to be loved.
  - I choose to let you love me.
  - I let you love me; on your terms, not mine.
  - I am fulfilled when I have experienced love.
  - I am now able to love others out of my own fulfillment.

- "I don't need you" is the language of the wounded heart.

- Needs give us the capacity to be loved and to feel loved.

- The degree to which I *let* you love me is the degree to which you *can* love me, no matter how much love you have for me.

- Trusting God's perfect love for us pushes away our fear and teaches us to embrace the love that heals our wounds.

- Love completely satisfies our longings, ambitions, and potential.

- When the requirements of our souls—our needs—are met, it satisfies us.

CHAPTER EIGHT

The Sweetest Gift of Grace: Repentance

Many have the space of repentance, who have not the grace of repentance.
—William Secker

Few of us would call repentance the "sweetest gift." For most of us repentance has been neither a gift nor sweet. A more fit analogy, in our minds, would be to compare repentance to a bitter-tasting cough syrup. We know we need to take it to cure our cough, but we hate it. It tastes like liquid linoleum! So we avoid it as long as possible, in hopes that our cough will simply heal itself. When it gets worse, and only as a last resort, we force it down.

When we don't know how to deal with our sin, we will try to hide it. That's why *The Room of Good Intentions* turns into such a masquerade ball. It's dress-up time! We know what we've done . . . we know what we *do*. And no amount of sadness, striving, or penance has done anything but compound our sadness. What we really need is a way home. We've been told to confess our sin, but we don't like that answer. We want to do something! Besides, we've confessed our sin a thousand times before, and what good did it do?

But when we walk around with unresolved sin, it's as if we're wearing a heavily insulated parka on the hottest day of the summer . . . in the Sahara! We're suffocating and can't figure out why. Repentance is the zipper out of that parka.

In the middle of our misery, Jesus taps us on the shoulder and says, "I have something for you that cost me everything to get for you. Here, it's a gift of my grace for you." Written across the gift is one word: *repentance*. The attached card reads: "Take it, apply it, and trust me to make it real. I love you. Jesus."

Some may question, "How can repentance be a gift if I am the one who's doing the repenting?" It is a gift of God's grace because your repentance literally doesn't have a chance without grace. Grace alone resolves sin. Grace alone heals, and grace alone gives power over sin. Only the power of the cross can break a pattern of sinful behavior. That's what makes repentance a gift that only Jesus can give. No one else died to bring us such power.

Willpower Is No Power

Yet many of us act as if repentance is a matter of the will. It's not. We cannot make a decision to stop sinning. We can't "will" ourselves into change. We can't "will" ourselves into feeling contrition or remorse. Repentance isn't doing something about our sin; rather, it means admitting that we *can't* do anything about our sin. We cannot woo ourselves into anything but the most external form of repentance.

All of our effort, striving, and willpower have only momentary, external value when it comes to fighting an opponent as crafty, intentional, persistent, powerful, and experienced as sin. To confirm this, we only have to look at all the legalistic Judaizers and Pharisees who've ever walked this earth. They believe they are godly because they have the willpower to deal with certain sin-related behaviors. Yet Jesus condemns them for trusting in themselves and having contempt for others.[1]

Understand this: The *intention* not to sin is not the same as the *power* not to sin. God did not design us to conquer sin on our own. To think we can is an incalculable *under*valuing of sin's power combined with a huge *over*valuing of our own willpower!

A Classic Oxymoron: Sin Management

Unfortunately, some of us fool ourselves into believing we can manage our sin, because we can stop from doing some things. Sometimes we learn to pick up our clothes after multiple reprimands . . . or we stop drinking diet soda after friends and relatives keep warning us of the ingredients . . . or we start driving the speed limit after our fifth speeding ticket. We think that because our will was sufficient enough to change some habits, we can tackle the big dog of sin.

Sin cannot be managed. If we make this our goal in repentance, we are doomed to fail. Think back to what we've said about motives, values, and actions. Our goal isn't to solve all of our sin issues. Our motive is to trust God so we can live out of who God says we are . . . so that *together* we can work on our sin issues. When we try to manage our sin through willpower, the process looks something like this:

Sin . . . confess . . . do better for a while, then sin again. Embarrassment, confess again, ask God to take away the desire, then sin again, confess again, sin again, confess again, shock, more determination to stop sinning, think about it a lot, examine it. Make promises, create some boundaries, and sin again, now even worse than before. Despair, anger, shame, distance from God, guilt. Self-condemnation, self-loathing . . . sin again. Disillusionment, doubt, self-pity, resentment at God: *Why doesn't he hear my prayers? Why doesn't he do something?* More anger. Then fear that we allow ourselves to get angry with God. Then real confession, a heartfelt one, and a sense of cleansing. Ah, a new start. Things seem better. *Yeah, I've finally got this sin under control.* Oops, sin again. Desperate efforts, bargains struck. Once-and-for-all healing. Really mean it this time. Sin again. Lose hope, give up, rationalize, minimize, blame, pull away, hide, judge others, put on a mask, go past the sin again, and so on.

This scenario, in varying degrees, depicts the pattern many Christians live out all their lives. This roller coaster ride has no happy ending. It only causes us to feel beaten down, to compromise our integrity, to feel cynical about this second-class life we lead.

Worse, a sin management system shuts off the *only resource* that can deal with sin: our *trust* in who God says we are, attracting the *power* of his *grace*.

Confession Is Limited

Confession does not resolve our sin either. To be sure, admitting our sin is an important part of the process—but words do not resolve sin. We can be sorry for something we have done wrong, and even confess it, and still desire to continue doing it. Agreeing that we have done something wrong is not the same as trusting God with what we have done. Confession is not the same as truly needing God to free us of the sin we have done. Sin is resolved when we are cleansed of it, and only dependence upon the cross of Jesus cleanses us from sin.[2] There is power there.

How does grace make repentance a gift for us—a gift that actually resolves our sin issues?

Grace-Empowered Repentance

When grace introduces us to repentance, the two of us become best friends. When anything else introduces us to repentance, it feels like the warden has come to lock us up. But when grace gets involved, the truths of repentance reveal a fabulous world of life-freeing beauty. What, then, are the truths of repentance that grace produces?

First, repentance is about trusting, not willing. Yes, there is choice involved, but if our *motive* is determined straining to please God, all our striving will be a pile of filthy rags.[3] We can do nothing—absolutely nothing—to make provision for our sin. In repentance we depend on God to turn water into wine. Trust in our act of repentance releases the gift of God's grace to transform our hope into reality.

What does trust attract? Grace, in the form of power, which comes to us *directly* from God's Spirit and then *indirectly* through others. A striver cannot access this power. We cannot quantify this power, but we can measure it—in the people who actually turn away from their previous path of destruction.

Remember, trusting God with ourselves allows us to receive love—his love and the love of others. And because we're loved, we can face what we have done to others and ourselves without having to retreat to a cave of hiddenness. Love acts as a safety net that can keep us from destruction as we admit the truth about ourselves. We know that nothing we do can change how God sees us. We also realize that there are people who will not change their assessment of our worth or the commitment of their love. Grasping that single truth makes us alive with creativity and risk, safe in the strong arms of real acceptance. We stop looking over our shoulder, waiting for that shoe we always feared was about to drop. Love catches the shoe on its way down . . . every time.

When we feel safe, we are much more disposed to open our hearts to God. When we feel safe, we let go of our self-defense and call out to him, saying, "God, I no longer have anything to prove. I have nothing to hold on to. I want only what you want for me." At that instant, we know we did not create such a response. God, in his grace, gave it to us when we chose to trust him. He graced our hearts; he gave the power; he will give the strength.

Many, many Christians do not trust God in the process of repentance. They view repentance as something they *should* do, but this preempts the power. Perhaps they have been taught that when they sin, they need only confess it, to agree it's wrong. But what's missing is the hope of it being defeated.

Every act of repentance depends on an act of redemption. *To redeem* means "to liberate by payment or to release from debt or blame."[4] Willpower, no matter how sincere, cannot buy you this freedom. There is no dealing with any sin without a redemptive act.

Bill was thirty years old and had been a Christian for thirteen years when he learned what a powerful gift repentance can be. Nobody needed to tell him that he had sin issues in his life, but one night he saw the devastating effect of what that sin was doing to him and those he loved. He had just lost his job, his reputation was damaged, and he was in the worst financial trouble of his life. Yet his internal life was even worse:

> I struggled with pornography. I compromised my integrity because I wanted to look good instead of telling the truth. I blamed others for what happened to my career. It was their fault we didn't have enough money. I knew a lot of it had to do with some bad choices on my part, and yet I couldn't admit that, in my deep insecurity.

Bill didn't understand how to be relieved of those sins. Looking back, he can see that his honest confession to his wife, Grace, three years earlier had opened a door for the Holy Spirit to sharpen his awareness for his need to repent of what was true about him. Grace's love offered Bill a place of safety and acceptance that invited him to trust even more.

Even though he had been a Christian for years, Bill had never realized it was possible that every sin he committed and every sin that had been done to him could be redeemed and healed. And, he didn't know what repentance had to do with it. The truth that Bill kept hearing on this night was, "As you have received the Lord Jesus Christ, so walk in him."[5] Bill faced the life-changing reality that there is *no difference* between the power to save and the power to resolve sin. Jesus could release him from the power of the sin that had such an immense hold on his life. By God's grace, he did and he does. God was healing Bill then, when he received Christ, and he is healing him now. But healing requires Bill to face God with what is true about him and to trust God to cleanse him. Bill had brought his sin to the Lord many, many times before. What was different about that night?

I stopped walking down that road of self-effort. I realized that confessing had only brought temporary relief. That night I walked off the well-worn path of *Pleasing God* and started walking down the road of *Trusting God*. Childlike trust pleases God most.

When we repent through trust, it is exclusively and entirely a gift of God's grace. That's where the power is. This kind of repentance actually provides a real power over sin. The work of Jesus is for every sin, not just for the forgiveness of that sin, but for the healing *from* that sin.[6]

What Inhibits Repentance?

So why is it that we can say, "This time, God, I really mean it" and yet not see resolution for our sin? By now you know that people in *The Room of Good Intentions* hold radically different assumptions about how to handle sin than those in *The Room of Grace.* The environment of the first room actually inhibits repentance, while the second one releases it. Notice three specific inhibitors of repentance.

Isolation. In *The Room of Good Intentions,* we don't want others to know about our sin. We want to keep our sin private, between God and us. Many times we begin to trust our own assessment of how we are doing with God. In our private thoughts, we establish our own benchmarks for godliness. If you are still attracted to this approach, revisit chapters two through four.

When our "repentance" functions in isolation rather than in community, it almost always indicates that we remain more concerned about personal appearances than the resolution of sin. We don't want people to think we are ungodly—to think less of us. The fact that our sin remains hidden from others proves we still favor presenting a nicely packaged life to others, while keeping sin quasi-managed and submerged. Yet, genuine repentance desires to resolve *anything* and *everything* about our sin. No cover, no posturing, just pure repentance. God built that desire into the gift.[7]

Pride. When our environment values striving to please God, we won't welcome repentance as a gift. Why? We've too much to prove to God, others, and ourselves. If we publicly repent, others will know that we have not done very well in our striving. That would be like getting a C– in godliness. Better to spin the truth a bit and tell others we are doing well. Better yet, point out ways in which others have messed up. That takes the focus off of us, moving us precariously close to the precipice of an unrepentant spirit. Pride—trust in ourselves—edges out repentance. Then, as Henry and Richard Blackaby write, "Pride will do what sin does. It destroys."[8]

Wrong Motive. In the event that we attempt repentance in *The Room of Good Intentions*, it will be out of a motive to make God happy with us, to become more godly. When we speak bold words of determined striving to please God, those words do not spring out of a motive of *trusting* God. It is so easy to relapse into that willpower kick. It's us trying to impress God again, without his grace. But trying to repent without grace is like trying to swim without water.

Resolute striving to *please* God begets a *pride* that keeps us focused on our own "power"—which is not a power to write home about. In contrast, repentance that comes from God is outfitted with otherworldly power—potency secured by Jesus' death and activated by his resurrection. Repentance is formidable against sin *only* because of actual power—the power of the cross. Our words or religious techniques have nothing to do with it. The power in this gift reminds us of the power in the ark of the covenant, a power so mighty that the Hebrews dared not come in contact with it.[9] The same power that resided in the ark is the power in this gift. But now, God invites us to come near his grace-wrapped power.

When we receive this sweet gift of repentance, a force is unleashed that can transform our hardened, contemptuous, alienated hearts into the most tender, loving, and gentle of souls. The word *sweet* has synonyms like "gratifying," "satisfying," and "fulfilling." They aptly define repentance. How sweet it is![10]

The Mindset of a Grace-Filled Community

By now, we understand why the community of good intentions experiences far less repentance than the community of grace. When we venture in that direction, we will do so without the grace needed to resolve our sin. Yet, in a grace-filled community, a different view of life in God biases the whole culture toward repentance. For starters, this community *expects* and *anticipates* imperfection. Yes, we honor others in the community as saints, but we also face the reality of each other's sin. We applaud vulnerability and view godliness as something much more than the presence of good behavior and the absence of bad behavior. We're too busy dancing to hold on to that dead weight. The individuals in this community trust God to mature them from the inside out, by the power of his Spirit . . . in his timing. No one feels a need to hide, for no one's parading his or her own righteousness. Everyone feels safe to be real and alive.

In such a community, repentance is as accessible to its members as fast food is to city dwellers. This community keeps repentance handy in the cupboard, ready to draw on its grace-power at a moment's notice. This group wouldn't go to bed at night without embracing repentance to ensure ongoing healing and love. It's a community of saints, after all. Saints who sin.

Picture this. Into the community of grace comes a hurting, tired, broken-down saint who has spent all her Christian life in a community of folks with good intentions. She's plowed through a number of relationships and hurt a lot of people on the way to this door. Now she has stumbled into an environment filled with people for whom trusting God in repentance is a way of life.

What difference will this community make in her life? A mask-shattering difference—a miraculous, life-changing reformation. These folk treat her for who she is: a saint. They deal with her sin the way God deals with theirs: by standing with her, with their arms around her. They commit to loving her, and they begin to show her how to receive their love. They accept her. They choose to see her like Jesus does. They let her into their own lives.

So far, so good. But what happens when one day she confesses, "I have lied. I have hurt those closest to me. I have betrayed my husband. I've deceived all of you too." Oops. What does the community do now?

Do they cower from her? Tell her that what she did isn't that bad, that she'll get over it? Convince her she was probably right? Do they give her nonverbal signals that they don't approve of such revelations? No. After maybe one or more share their own story of failure, they tell her a new story about this beautiful gift used quite routinely in the community. Then, they ask her, "Do you remember how you've learned to receive love? You trusted God and others for it. Well, my friend, that's how you get this gift too. Just lean into God. Depend on what he tells you and trust his lead."

Don't you think this woman might actually try trusting God for his gift of repentance? In such environments repentance becomes a way of life. And, when that happens, grace heals, matures, reconciles, and unleashes the love of God through people. And the community of broken healers becomes more beautiful by the day. One day this woman stands near the door, waiting for the next wounded soul to stumble in, so she can be one of the first to tell the new story of this gift . . . a gift "used quite routinely in the community."

When failing strivers stumble into a community of grace, safety, and vulnerable repentance, it radically disrupts their game plan. Suddenly, they are face to face with a real, tangible option of sweet freedom. And the ongoing environment of the community tells them that they have not dreamed up this way of life. As the community treats them as they have never been treated before, their confidence grows that grace can support the full weight of their sin.

Repentance Will Set You Free

During his late teens, Bruce battled the dark-heartedness of "guilt trips" when he didn't live up to either his own or others' expectations of him. He wanted so much to prove himself to God and others. Drivenness would kick in during these seasons and, not surprisingly, his behavior hurt others and himself. Bruce says, "About that time, I could've really used a spiritual director like the one who told Brennan Manning, 'Brennan, give up trying to look good and sound like a saint. It will be a lot easier on everybody.'"[11] Even though Bruce tried his hardest, he could not break loose of this pattern. He wore out many pairs of shoes on the try-harder path of *Pleasing God*. Strange, how directions get confused—God didn't even want Bruce on that dangerous stretch of road, and Bruce was never quite convinced that his sold-out efforts of moral striving to make God happy and impress others were working. He grew exhausted struggling to overcome this pattern, while at the same time, devaluing the wounds he caused others.

During these months, deepening pain eventually prompted Bruce to self-reflection on power—the power of grace versus what he brought to the table. That season eventually freed Bruce into a powerful repentance that broke the old cycle and began a whole new life pattern. His words went something like this:

> All right, God, I cannot conquer this recurring sin. And it is
> hurting people. I will not build my life around creating a

security for myself that you've already secured. I trust your conclusion about me, not my own. Lord Jesus, I lean into your power for breaking this cycle.

"Leaning into" (trusting) these truths applied the power of the cross directly to Bruce's previously unbreakable pattern. Has Bruce ever relapsed onto the *Pleasing God* road? Oh, for sure. He knows that trail by heart. But, the cross—not Bruce's prayer, not his confession—powered a whole new way of living for Bruce. It is infinitely more relaxing, more freeing, and more maturing. He will not go back to that way of life.

When grace brings truth to light, it sometimes does so through love (as we learned in the last chapter), sometimes through forgiveness (as we'll learn in the next chapter), and sometimes through repentance. The principles of God's grace play off of each other. Grace begets repentance, and repentance nurtures forgiveness. Trust attracts grace, and grace helps saints to trust. Even goofed-up, compromised, failed, and confused saints. *Especially* them.

When repentance becomes a constant, recognizable part in an environment, the people in that culture experience freedom they never knew. They have amazing stories to tell. The truth always sets us free. Free to love God and others, free to trust even more truth, free to heal and reconcile, free to bring reconciliation to those who still don't know the Reconciler, free to follow our callings and dreams.

Learning to Trust Like We Did the First Time

Do we really trust God? Even more specifically, do we really believe the God we trust is strong enough and powerful enough to heal us? That is the bottom line. It may be easier to believe that Jesus died for all our sin so that we can go to heaven, somewhere out there in the distant future. But the power to heal habitual, present sin? Sin that's here and now; that's noisy, agonizing, hot, angry, and very, very real? We typically reason, *I think God will get me to heaven, but I'm really not sure he can handle this one.*

So, trusting God for his grace in repentance prompts us to ask:

- "God, are you strong enough to heal my patterns of self-destruction?"
- "God, do you always have my best interests at heart?"
- "God, are you able to take care of me if I live without the mask, if I walk around with no devices for self-protection?"
- "God, are you able to vindicate me if I do not vindicate myself?"
- "God, are you able to deal with my sin if I make the decision to turn away from my willpower to trusting in your power?"
- "God, are you able to protect me when in disclosure I am vulnerable to others knowing what is true about me?"

As we exercise our trust, we receive his grace. Just like we did the first time we met him.

Repentance at Any Age

John's daughter Amy is bright and alive and fun and beautiful. She is also stubborn and prone to her father's obsessive tendencies. Not too long ago, Amy broke the heart of a neat young man by allowing their relationship to move too quickly. At times Amy has been in love with the thought of being in love. After her emotions cool, she backs away to "just be friends." She did this with this particular young man, and it hurt him. We'll let John tell the story:

> I don't think I would've been bothered as a father so much except that I really liked this guy. He really liked her. And this was not her first time hurting a boy she liked. Amy had walked through this process twice before.
>
> So, one morning I took her out for breakfast at our neighborhood International House of Pancakes. I bumbled my way into sharing my concern about her relationships. She got defensive and aloof. She said she was sorry, but she also said, "What am I supposed to do, lie to him? I don't *feel* more than friends with him."
>
> I was sad because she was choosing to go it alone, reacting to stuff she didn't know how to fix, not letting anyone else in. I was sad because hurting others was hurting her and changing her. I was sad because I adore her and didn't want my daughter to live out a selfish pattern that would damage

her future. I was sad because she didn't see that Jesus was hurting for her. Somewhere in the middle of mixing eggs with my hash browns, I started to cry. Amy asked me what was wrong, and I told her all those things. And I told her how sad it must make Jesus to watch her bluff through life alone, reacting and repositioning.

Something beautiful happened in that moment: Trust awakened. Tears started welling up in Amy's eyes. She said, "I don't want to live like this anymore. I don't want to hurt anyone like this anymore. I don't want to do this to one more person. I don't want to hurt Jesus. I'm sorry, Dad. I feel so sad. I don't know how to do this any better. It's like I know the right thing to do, but when I get in certain situations I change the rules and do what I think will take care of Amy in that moment. I think I've been trying to do things on my own for so long, it's all I know. But I want God to help change me. Dad, will you help me?"

I reminded her that this was the reason Jesus came—so that she'd never have to live in the shame or embarrassment of failure. I reminded her that when we come face to face with our failure, Jesus is never closer to us. I reminded her that he is not ashamed of her. I reminded her that he was deeply proud of her for being vulnerable. I reminded her that this is the basis of why we worship—God loves us more than we can love ourselves and he can solve what we cannot. I told her that she was unable to change herself simply because she was sorry. But she could put her full trust and dependency in Jesus, and he would be faithful to change her, from the inside out.

That morning my precious daughter broke the pattern of an "I'm sorry" that gets parents off her back to an "I'm sorry" that demonstrated repentance. Amy was asking for more than forgiveness. She was trusting God to help her no longer hide behind an indifference that was merely a defense for her fear of rejection. That day she experienced the sweetest gift of grace. She learned a repentance that could take off her mask and allow the process of unresolved sin to be stopped in its tracks. In that moment, my precious daughter learned not to go it alone.

When trust awakens, grace is never far away. My daughter's repentance was real. God stood with Amy, her sin in front of them, and his grace empowered her. She went to this young man, told him how sorry she was for her careless-ness with his heart, and asked his forgiveness. She has main-tained a real and beautiful friendship with that young man. They care for each other and protect each other and periodi-cally write and phone each other. Amy's grace-infused repen-tance earned his trust. They will be friends for a long time.

In *The Room of Grace* no one is above anyone else. No one brags about his or her accomplishments. No one keeps score.

No one is shunned. No one can lose membership for blowing it. This room is not a utopian ideal. It is a home where people live together. One of them lives under my roof. Her name is Amy.

A Prayer for You

Don't dismiss the unstoppable force of repentance, or once again you'll resort to cheesecloth and bailing wire. When you are ready to trust God's provision for resolving your sin, you will pray something like this:

God, here we go. Here is a sin I trust you to do something about. I am convinced I cannot deal with this sin. I trust what you did at the cross is powerful enough, not only to bring me to heaven one day, but powerful enough that it can break this very sin's power that is now plaguing my life.

≡ DID YOU DISCOVER?

- Repentance is a gift of God's grace because your repentance resolves nothing without grace. Grace alone resolves sin.

- Only the power of the cross can break a pattern of sinful behavior.

- Repentance isn't doing something about our sin; rather, it means admitting that we *can't* do anything about our sin.

- Sin cannot be managed.

- A sin management system shuts off the *only* resource that can deal with sin: our *trust* in who God says we are, attracting the *power* of his *grace*.

- Agreeing that we have done something wrong is not the same as trusting God with what we have done.

- We can do absolutely nothing to make provision for our sin.

- Every act of repentance depends on an act of redemption.

- Three common inhibitors of repentance are isolation, pride, and a wrong motive.

- When grace brings truth to light, it sometimes does so through *love*, sometimes through *forgiveness*, and sometimes through *repentance*.

CHAPTER NINE

The Most Mysterious Gift of Grace: Forgiveness

Christianity is the only religion whose God bears the scars of evil.
—Os Guinness

Forgiveness breaks down walls, frees hearts, mends countries, restores families, and draws out the best in us. It can turn hatred into tenderness and the desire to destroy into a passion to protect. It is more powerful than any weapon, government, or wealth. Nothing else can bring such profound healing. Forgiveness forms the foundation of our relationship with God and sustains our relationships with each other. When we unleash this gift, by receiving it in humble trust that God can actually free our heart and heal our relationships, then the miraculous can happen. This powerful gift has one purpose: to protect us from the insidious harm that comes from *sin done against us.*

We need a way home. We've been told to get over the sin done to us, but we can't find our way out of the shadows. We can't seem to let go of our hurt. Then, in the middle of our misery, Jesus taps us on the shoulder and says, "I have something for you that cost me everything to get for you. Here, it's a gift of my grace for you." Written across the gift is one word: *forgiveness*. The attached card reads: "Take it, apply it, and trust me to make it real. I love you. Jesus. "

Forgiveness produces results so far out of our normal experience that it feels mysterious. Forgiveness brings alienated enemies together again. People who hated each other. People who do whatever they can never to see or talk to each other again. People who have pledged to kill each other. People who *have* killed each others' family members. When people forgive, their hearts are woven together in love. This is mysterious stuff.

A Teenager's Trauma

Near the end of Bill's first semester as a high-school freshman, some of his "friends" played a devastating practical joke on him. In between classes they took off his pants in the main stairwell where kids rushed from class to class. They called it "de-pants-ing." They held Bill down long enough for dozens of people to see him naked. He especially remembered the girls walking by. The de-pants-ing didn't last long, maybe less than a minute, but the scars lasted years. When Bill finally got away from his friends, he immediately started crying and ran home. He felt incredible sadness, pain, and shame. Even today Bill can vividly remember every single moment of that minute.

Sometime during that semester Bill's family moved to Arizona. Even though he was more than two thousand miles away from those who had hurt him, he couldn't forget what they had done. Now he was angry, and his anger had an immensely profound effect. Bill began to blame that experience for why he didn't know how to get along with girls. He'd lie in bed at night plotting the deaths of his friends. He even planned how to do it so no one would ever know the culprit.

In his shame, Bill blamed his classmates for who he was becoming. His inability to resolve what they did against him led to a horrible permission. Bill began to connect many of the issues of his developing sexuality to the embarrassment of that moment.

After high school, Bill became a Christian. He went to a Bible college and learned he needed to forgive these friends. When he forgave them, God truly healed Bill of the pain of that day. That summer he also forgave his offenders face to face. We'll let him tell you about it in his own words:

> I had a house-painting business in my old hometown, and I hired three of these guys to work for me. During lunch one day, we were all sitting under a tree. I said, "You know, guys, I have something really important I want to share with you. I'd like to talk about that time you de-pantsed me."
>
> Jim quickly answered, "That was you? Gosh, that was funny! We must have laughed about that for weeks." The other two guys laughed and all of them went back to their lunch. I just sat there, stunned. This was one of the most traumatic experiences of my life and they'd forgotten to whom they'd even done it!

Sin done against us profoundly affects us. Sometimes it can distort life and cause us to make some incredibly unhealthy judgments. After a while, these guys could tell that this memory was really important to me. Joe, Jim's brother said, "Hey, I'm sorry. We were just having fun. Is there anything we can do?"

Although it was awkward, I told them how that day had impacted me. I told them that my best friends should be the ones to protect me from an experience like that—they shouldn't have *initiated* it. I realized they'd never thought about most of what I was saying. I moved toward these guys in love and forgiveness. I needed to hear them say they were sorry, and when they told me they were, I believed they meant it, and I forgave them.

That summer Bill learned some unforgettable things about forgiveness. We'll use his story and a few others to help us understand the keys of forgiveness in their order.

KEY #1: Admit Something Happened!

God's provision for our healing always begins with our recognition that someone has sinned against us.

We often skip this first step in forgiveness for a variety of reasons. We may not realize that we have been sinned against. This is often the case when we are sinned against as a child—abused, neglected, demeaned, and so on.

Or, we may feel we will lose control of the relationship if we say we've been hurt. We think that if we don't admit it, no one will have any control over us—someone more articulate or powerful will not be able to manipulate us into believing we are the guilty party.

Or, we may want to deny that we have been hurt. We think, *This shouldn't bother me. I will just go on.* It may feel too fragile to admit we've been hurt. For example, in Bill's developing adolescence he could've determined he was just going to act tough, be macho, and say, "It was nothing. Didn't bother me at all." Fortunately, he admitted the hurt, or forgiveness would never have occurred.

We cannot forgive *until* we admit we have been sinned against. This does not mean we should start searching for all the things we haven't acknowledged were done against us. We're talking about the things we *know* have been done against us that we've chosen to deny. These offenses nag at us, and most will surface automatically. This is an invitation to stop hiding the sin that someone else has done against us. To forgive, we must admit what is already true.

KEY #2: Forgive the Consequences of the Act Done Against You

Often the consequences of the act done against us are worse—sometimes far worse—than the act of sin itself.

This was true for Bill . . . and it was true for Bruce. One of the most traumatic seasons in his life occurred when several leaders lied to him and then about him to others. He says:

> My struggle was not in forgiving these leaders for the dishonesty. I understand how false statements get made. They seem mild compared to the substantial consequences of those lies — the loss of reputation, friends, finances, and some of my dreams. These were much more heart wrenching than the lies themselves. I needed to forgive more than the dishonesty and betrayal. Only when I got in touch with the impact that the dishonesty had on my life was I able to trust God in forgiving these leaders for the specific things I held against them: the *consequences* of their sin against me. Without forgiving for the consequences of the lying, I could not experience healing, freedom, and reconciliation. Being freed from just the act of sin would've left me bound to the consequences.

In order to understand the effect a sin has had on us, we find it helps to write down the incident and what happened. But we can't stop there. We need to include how the incident impacted our life, to get in touch with how we felt as a result of that event. We need to ask ourselves questions like these: Did I experience shame? Did I become fearful? Did I feel demeaned and devalued? Did anger and resentment begin to grow within me? Did I feel manipulated? Was I shunned?

Were there relational effects? Did I lose my marriage, my children, my friends? Did I lose a business or a sum of money? Did I lose my position or leadership role? Has this sin led to a change in my outlook or attitude toward life?

As we allow ourselves to feel the pain of our responses, we begin to understand the consequences of the sin done to us. This is critical. Harboring enables the sin that was committed against us to define us.[1] Remember, unresolved sins are buried alive, including the ones done against us. This hard work prepares us to forgive.

KEY #3: Tell God What Happened to You

Once we have acknowledged what has happened and how it affected us, we must pour out our hearts to God, telling him everything about what happened to us.

We might think he doesn't want to hear it all, but we would be wrong. We might think, *No way! This is only for emotionally based people. I don't do that stuff.* But we would be very wrong. We might think that we should be past this, and that any rehearsal of the event is akin to wallowing in it, but we would be wrong. We might think that because God already knows these things, he doesn't want to hear them again from us, but we would be wrong.

We can mumble, cry, sigh, get angry, shout, run around the room, howl like a coyote if we need to—but let's not stop short of getting in touch with all the effects and feelings inside us from that person's sin against us. We shouldn't stop until we're sure we've told God everything that happened to us. Everything.

When Bill came to the realization of the power of forgiveness, he forgave his friends for taking off his pants in the stairwell and holding him down. It took him much longer to tell God about the feelings of shame and the pain, about the multiple nights of dreaming of their demise, about his anger, about his self-consciousness, about his blaming them for the inability to date girls. But in time he got it all out. We need to do the same.

KEY #4: Forgive the Offender for Your Benefit

Forgiveness has an order—we must initiate the *vertical transaction* with God before we move into the *horizontal transaction* with others. First, before God, we forgive the offenders for what they've done and the consequences it has reaped in our life. This is between God and us, *for our sake.*[2] Then, after we've forgiven our offenders before God, we go to our offender and forgive him or her. We'll call that a *horizontal transaction.* If we don't get this right, if we move toward the person without having been cleansed before God, we risk moving toward our offender in bitterness, resentment, judgment, and a spirit of getting even. If we prematurely attempt reconciliation with the offender, we'll bring the residue of unresolved sin into the equation. And everyone can smell it. Trusting becomes harder than peddling an angry bear uphill on a unicycle.

If we try to go on without forgiving the one who hurt us before God, or if we say, "I'm not going to repent until they repent," we end up in bitterness, anger, resentment, or jealousy. In our unwillingness to forgive before God, we become the issue.[3]

It's helpful to see ourselves lifting this sin and all its consequences to God, to see ourselves laying the entire deal in his hands. Does this take trust? You bet it does. That's why we're on the road of *Trusting God*. In an act of trust, we hand over the responsibility of what to do next to our fully wise, good, trustworthy, and just Lord. We fully acknowledge the wrong done to us, and we place both the act and the consequences into his hands. The whole incident—the facts, thoughts, feelings, judgments, and resulting pain—moves out of our sphere into God's.

How will we know if we've forgiven someone? When we know we can offer that person our love. When forgiveness stays only in our minds and doesn't sink deep into our hearts, it cannot be effective.

Like repentance, forgiveness is a matter of the heart. The act genuinely clears the mind and emotions of sin and all its effects in us. Bill forgave his friends before God long before he hired them to work for him and had that face-to-face meeting. On that day *they* received his forgiveness. But Bill had experienced the benefits of forgiving them long before they heard him say, "I forgive you."

When we forgive, first vertically and then horizontally, it's like huge cement bags have been lifted off our shoulders. It makes us ready to love again, and that prepares us for the next key.

KEY #5: Forgive the Offender When They Repent, for Their Sake

Forgiving the person before God releases us of judgment, bitterness, and resentment toward our offender. When we forgive, our heart heals and we are ready to forgive the one who hurt us—person to person—for that person's sake.

Whew, doggies! This is one of those incredible times when the benefits of trusting God are visibly and profoundly mysterious and miraculous. Such is the miracle of God's grace in our heart.

Yet to go to another and declare "I forgive you" before that person repents does nothing for the relationship and robs the offender of the opportunity for his or her own life-freeing repentance. God uses repentance to heal sinful hearts. We shouldn't deprive our offender of that gift. Our forgiveness will not free the other person from their offense, nor will it heal our relationship, if it is premature. The one who sinned against us must repent for his or her own sake—to be healed from sin. Upon the other person's repentance, we can forgive.

We forgive our offender with the goal of restoring the relationship, not just resolving the conflict. We desire our offender's repentance, not to hold it over him or her, but so we can continue on in a healthy relationship. Their repentance won't heal our heart—that is what happens when we forgive our offender before God. But their repentance will heal our *relationship*.

We can pursue reconciliation, but we can't force it. We can't demand repentance. As you may remember from chapter eight, repentance requires a heart that trusts God. That's a grace-room moment. Our insistence that another repent has no sway in the matter.

Have you ever noticed that Jesus waits for our repentance before he forgives us? Think about it. On the cross he cried out, "Father, forgive them."[4] If that cry was for *our* sake, then everyone gets forgiven, receives salvation, and goes to heaven, regardless of their decision of repentance. We know that isn't the case. On the cross Jesus asked the Father to forgive those who had crucified him, for *his* own sake, that he would not be contaminated by the sin done against him. Jesus on the cross demonstrates key number five. When we repent of our sins against God and ask for his forgiveness, then and only then does he forgive us and reconcile us to himself. When we repent, Jesus grants forgiveness for our sake.

When we forgive the offender, for his or her sake, it prepares the way for the relationship to be restored.

When we allow God to heal us from being sinned against, we get to turn around and help those who have sinned against us to find healing from their sin! How amazing!

KEY #6: Distinguish Between Forgiving and Trusting Your Offender

As forgiveness prepares the way for the relationship to be restored, it is important to understand that forgiveness does not mean we have to trust the other person yet. This misunderstanding causes many to balk at forgiveness. Because they can't trust the person, they believe they can't forgive him or her. But forgiving the person and trusting the person again are always separate issues. Even if we have forgiven our offender—even if our offender has repented and asked our forgiveness—we will still, in the future, have to deal with the issue of mutual trust. Trustworthiness must be evaluated. Our expectations should be realistic because while trust is easily broken, it is recovered very slowly, and sometimes not at all. Forgiveness carries the hope of renewed trust in the offender, but it does not mandate or guarantee it. For example, when sin violates the commitment of marriage, the offender can be and should be forgiven, but the restoration of the trust necessary to re-honor the commitment takes time.

KEY #7: Seek Reconciliation, Not Just Conflict Resolution

When we help someone say, "Will you forgive me?" we engage that person in the relationship. Reconciliation belongs to a completely different stratosphere than mere conflict resolution. Most of us want to settle for just fixing the conflict. So we use terms like, "I'm sorry that happened," or "I really made a mistake on *that* one." When we are willing to say, "Will you forgive me because I did _____?" we create the opportunity for people to forgive us and sometimes even come back into heart relationship with us.

As recreation director at a day-care center, John felt like he was the Henry Kissinger of playground diplomacy when he forced two eight-year-old boys in conflict to apologize to each other. In his most authoritative playground director's voice, John said, "All right, what happened here?" Not a great question to ask if you want an honest answer. (What would you answer? "Well, sir, I cheated at baseball and called Kevin out when he was safe. Then I hit him in the leg with the baseball bat. Before he had a chance to react I got him in a headlock and was about to gouge his eyes out when you showed up.")

After listening to both of their versions, which were oddly different, and after hearing a dozen distinct versions from the assembled mob, John recalls, "I knew I would not be able to render a just verdict, so I said, 'All right, Trevor. I want you to apologize to Kevin. And Kevin, I want you to forgive Trevor.' They looked at me as though I had said, 'Kids, I want you to find a mule and take it bowling.' Solitary confinement they could have understood and obeyed. Sweeping the breezeway for a year would have made sense. But apologizing and forgiving? On what basis? Neither was sorry and neither was ready to forgive someone who wasn't sorry.

"But their lack of readiness didn't stop me. I pushed, saying, 'I mean it—now!' Trevor mumbled, 'I'm sorry,' and Kevin muttered, 'I forgive you.' By forcing them to do something they didn't believe, I caused them to betray themselves. And, by forcing a request for insincere forgiveness, I kept these kids from honestly facing what they had done wrong. I kept them both from an opportunity to be made right with the other."

In our anxiousness to fix conflicts, we sometimes push people to say they are sorry. But have you noticed that people don't get fixed or stay fixed when we try to force it? Grace always invites rather than demands reconciliation. An apology may make the issue go away for the present time, but it won't heal the relationship. Remember—that's what forgiveness always seeks. Jesus paid with his life to bring us reconciliation. This is sacred ground.

Mystery in The Room of Grace

A distinguished draftsman, engineer, artist, and thinker, Leonardo da Vinci is one of the outstanding intellects of history. Just before he started painting *The Last Supper*, he had a violent quarrel with a fellow painter. Enraged and bitter, Leonardo determined to paint the face of his enemy—the other artist—as the face of Judas and thus take out his revenge by sending this man down in infamy. Judas was one of the first faces he painted, and everyone recognized the face of the painter with whom Leonardo had quarreled.

But when Leonardo came to paint the face of Christ, he could make no progress. Something was holding him back, frustrating his best efforts. Eventually, he came to the conclusion that the thing checking and frustrating him was that he had painted his enemy as Judas. He decided to paint out the face of Judas and start fresh on the face of Jesus. He did, and this time with the success which the ages have acclaimed.[5]

Leonardo experienced the power and genius of grace. He had discovered a universal truth: We cannot simultaneously paint the features of Christ into our life and paint another face with the colors of enmity and hatred.

Where does God stand in relation to the sin done against us when we live in *The Room of Grace?* He stands *with* us. He has his arm around us, giving us his perspective on the sin and the one who sinned. He's close enough for us to hear him say, "If you ask me—and I hope you do—you should forgive this person as my Son forgave you. Trust me with this advice, and I'll heal you, restore you, and free you with the truth it brings to you."

God stands with us in *The Room of Grace* because we trusted him. He says, "You believe that I have made you a saint. Now, live as one. My son died to reconcile you. That was my ultimate Gift to you. It made possible this mysterious power—the gift of forgiveness. Please value it as I do. Forgive those who have sinned against you."

God has given us three gifts beyond explaining. The best gift we can give back to God is our trust.[6] Trust him with the forgiveness issues in your life.

⚏ DID YOU DISCOVER?

- The powerful gift of forgiveness has one main purpose: to protect us from the insidious harm that comes from *sin done against us*.

- God's provision for our healing always begins with our recognition that someone has sinned against us.

- There is a sequence for forgiveness to resolve sin.

- To forgive, we must first admit what is already true.

- We forgive the offenders in our lives for what they've done and its consequences in our life. This is between God and us, *for our sake*.

- Forgiving others for the consequences of their sin against us is usually much more difficult than the sin itself.

- Forgiving the person before God releases us of judgment, bitterness, and resentment toward our offender.

- We forgive our offender with the goal of restoring the relationship, not just resolving the conflict.

- When we forgive the offender for his or her sake, it prepares the way for the relationship to be restored.

- Forgiveness carries the hope of renewed trust in the relationship, but it does not mandate or guarantee it. Forgiving and trusting are not the same thing.

- Grace always invites rather than demands reconciliation.

CHAPTER TEN

Maturing into God's Dreams for You

For the longest time I used to think that my major contribution to the Body of
Christ would be my attendance at potlucks.
—Bob Ryan

$\equiv$ Ever since we were children we have had dreams and hopes of destiny. Some of these dreams are our own, but others came from the very hand of God—and God's dreams never go off the radar screen. Even time, failure, or heartbreak can't make us forget them entirely. Still, most of us have tried to stuff them into the attic. We have been rudely awakened out of too many of them, too many times, and each time we lost more and more of the dream. Yet even if we've forgotten the fiber of those dreams, God has not.

God dreams that you would discover your destiny and walk into the reasons he placed you on this earth. God has a ticket of destiny with your name written on it—no matter how old, how broken, how tired, or how frightened you are. No matter how many times you may have failed, God dearly longs for the day when he gets to hand you that ticket, smile, and whisper into your ear, "You have no idea how long I've waited to hand this to you. Have a blast! I've already seen what you get to do. It's better than you could have dreamed. Now hurry up and get on that train. A whole lot of folk are waiting for you to walk into your destiny and into their lives."[1]

In this chapter we want to show you the hope that comes from living in *The Room of Grace*. We will offer a few crucial observations on maturity—what hinders it and what promotes it. Then we will introduce you to two friends who have met the ticket puncher in the back of *The Room of Grace*, where trains leave all the time, taking us into God's dream for us.

All aboard!

What Hinders God's Dream for Us?

People in *The Room of Good Intentions* never get released into the dreams God has for them. Everyone here is trying to change into someone else to appease God. We hide, position, strive, perfect our self-effort, and polish our image. We often interpret our ability to compete well against each other as a sign of our godliness and success. We look very impressive—we have learned to package our techniques well—but our self-effort keeps us self-centered and immature.

As we said in chapter 2, whenever we are trapped in shame or blame or anger, for any period of time, we stop maturing. This is what happens when we lodge in *The Room of Good Intentions*. We may become competent and skilled. We may achieve position and significant-looking roles. We do stuff—maybe even impressive stuff. But, because we are constantly pursuing power and authority, and manipulating to gain control, God can never release us into our future. Our relational sadness, our inability to be loved, our festering wounds and broken relationships freeze us in immaturity. Without humility, we continue to miss the train that takes us into God's intention for our destiny.

There is no *releasing* without *maturing*.

There is no maturing without *healing*.

There is no healing without *gifts of grace*.

There are no gifts of grace outside *The Room of Grace*.

There is no *Room of Grace* without a door marked *Living Out of Who God Says I Am*, opened with a doorknob of *Humility*.

There is no humility without choosing to walk a road called *Trusting God*.

Only then do I learn how God stands with me to resolve my sin.

Growing into Maturity in The Room of Grace

We who dwell in *The Room of Grace* have come to believe who God says we are. We're not trying to change into another person. God has made us exactly who he wants us to be, and we have come to believe it. Any change that takes place in us comes from *maturing* into the person we already are—much like a caterpillar matures into a butterfly.

Jesus is the Son of God. As man, he matured in God's perfect timing for release into the astonishing destiny God had for him. Jesus did not try to change to be better in order to please his Father. He already knew that his Father was well pleased with him.[2] Instead, he constantly entrusted himself to the Father so that he could mature.[3] We are told to emulate Jesus' pattern of entrusting himself to his Father.[4]

In *The Room of Grace* we learn to trust, to wait, to rest in God's promises, to grow in health and authentic relationships, so we will mature toward the day of God's releasing us into our destiny.[5] We don't pursue power, authority, or office. We wait to receive God's authority, his exaltation of the humble. We patiently wait for God to give us the desires of our hearts.[6] We're no longer in a hurry. We know he cares about our destiny more than us. We know he has already seen the day of our release. It makes us smile like remembering a secret shared between best friends.

The mature in this room have also learned how to live with a community of people who trust God and others with what is true about them. We—and the others in this community—have taken off our masks and are learning to walk in the resplendent freedom and purposes of God. But, we remember the pain of letting go of our masks; we still carry the scars from where the glue tore our skin.

We are not free from visible problems and issues just because we no longer hide them. Our issues are there for everyone to see. Sometimes the mature homeowners in *The Room of Grace* appear to have more issues than the prize citizens of *The Room of Good Intentions*.

We depend upon God and his power and resources. We are free to trust him for repentance. We are free to trust him so we can forgive others and be forgiven.

Most of all, the mature have a childlike joy and freedom. We are playfully alive and will never allow anyone to return us to hiding. We may be tempted to stumble back into the empty promises of *The Room of Good Intentions,* but that lure carries less and less power as we mature in *The Room of Grace.* We have tasted too much life to want to leave this room. We know too much; we've drunk deeply of the grace of God. It has blanketed us like wool and hot cocoa on a cold night. We are part of the growing neighborhood of those who've chosen to believe who God says we are.

But such maturity does not happen overnight. God uses many others for our benefit in this process. Some are teachers, counselors, friends, pastors, spouses, siblings, children, mentors, disciplers, spiritual guides, and spiritual directors.[7]

Spiritual disciplines are practiced in *The Room of Grace* as part of the process of maturing and releasing the saint to minister the gospel of the kingdom. These disciplines are no longer seen as a means of entry to *The Room of Grace.* "They are disciplines designed to help us be active and effective in the spiritual realm of our own heart, now spiritually alive by grace in relationship to God and his kingdom."[8]

Growing in Maturity

Maturity in *The Room of Grace* occurs in three general phases. Of course, these phases overlap each other, and we often jump back and forth in our development. But for the sake of clarity, we are making each phase more distinct than it actually is in experience.

Phase One: Healing the Needy Christian

As we have pointed out, everyone who walks into *The Room of Grace* initially is *me-centered.* In this room we learn some foundational, essential truths: We become acquainted with the power of love and grace and truth; we identify the various wounds we carry; we embrace the significance of our new identity; we discover relational principles. We also discover the process of unresolved sin issues as well as the cycle and power of sin. We are immersed in the person and work of Jesus, the Holy Spirit, and the Father.

But if we remain in this phase, we will stagnate and grow cynical because we are not applying the truths we are learning. We need not rush through this phase, however; it's important not to force application before we understand what we are applying. Such is a breeding ground for self-effort.

One of the greatest gifts we can offer another person is a safe place to fail. In this room, teachers and mentors help youthful followers of Christ to learn the priority of not hiding. This is such a place—a room where they can disclose what is really true about the sin in them and the sin that has been done against them. Such a gift at this phase in a believer's life is profound and freeing.

Young, maturing believers adapt themselves to others' expectations, real or imagined. So, we want to make sure our expectations match

God's expectations. If they don't and others try to meet our inappropriate expectations, we actually thwart their maturity. So, we model and
teach truth about who they are in Christ; who God says they are. As you
know by now, it isn't enough to know what the Bible says about who we
are in Christ. We must actually live it. We do well to hang around real
people who are living it. This is how we nurture maturity in another.

Phase Two: Maturing the Healing Christian

In time we become more *others-centered*. In the last stage, the emphasis
was on introduction and new awareness of truth. In this stage we focus
with others on applying, developing, and processing the truths we
learned in phase one. For example, we learn to apply love, grace, and
truth to our life situation and circumstances, and so our wounds begin
to heal. We begin living out of our new identity and applying truth to
the dynamics of sin. We begin to experience in real relationships the
relational principles we are learning, and we understand that what we
are learning is not just something we know, but something we are experiencing as truth. We are developing a vitally wonderful relationship
with Jesus, the Holy Spirit, and the Father. In this phase, we are looking
around our world and beyond to see how God wants us to love others.

This stage more fully introduces the reality of suffering. Not the suffering from sickness, accidents, or unfortunate circumstances, but the
suffering that comes from aligning ourselves with truth, with truth-
telling. God uses suffering to mature the humble as they come under his
influence and obey his truth, out of a heart of love. As they grow in trust

during this suffering, God will enlarge their sphere of influence, because the humble can be trusted with truth.

At this stage we are looking for and encouraging vulnerability, made evident by our new level of authenticity. We no longer hide. We don't arrive at this stage by taking an eight-week series or a class. Maturity is a process; it takes time. Don't rush the pace it takes for character to mature.

Phase Three: Releasing the Maturing Christian

In this third stage, our life becomes more *Christ-centered*. We *naturally* respond to life out of our new identity—a Christlike identity—that we live through grace and truth. Our past wounds no longer identify us, and we experience freedom in our new identity. We no longer live under the control of sin. We are experiencing the power of community and relational vulnerability. And, maybe best of all, we live as an intimate friend of Jesus. We mature into a beautiful, trusting dependency upon the Holy Spirit and walk into the purposes of God the Father. In this stage we are looking around our world and beyond to see how God wants us to love others through his particular plans and destiny for us.

We gauge maturity by how we live with others who are maturing. Mature Christians delight in God's exaltation of others. We do not fear others' strengths; we understand them, submit to them, and benefit from them. The mature influence others, not so much out of the power of their position, but out of their person. We receive power; we don't pursue it. We focus on influence, not on opportunities that might compromise our convictions.

We make decisions primarily for the benefit of others and are willing to suffer so that others might mature. We receive our destiny from God's hand. We learn to own and take responsibility for our influence. We accept the cost of commitment that comes with someone trusting us. The mature enjoy God's protection and his jealous love for them. We offer to others that same kind of protective love and receive it from others. The mature ask the exhilarating question fashioned by Ken Gire, "What dream is God dreaming when He dreams about you and about me, and how can we help that dream come true?"[9] The mature are always learning, studying, and inviting others to speak into our lives and meet our needs.[10]

Does this sound too good to be true? Believe us—it is not. In fact, it even gets better.

Receiving the Dream

And then the day comes. For some, the release feels premature; for others, the wait is agonizingly long. But all have learned to believe it would arrive. Life in *The Room of Grace* teaches us to wait for God's exaltation, rather than to pursue position or power.[11] It's always the perfect time. For one thing, our dreams are being clarified as our sin is being resolved, our wounds are being healed, and we are in the process of maturing. Our lives are no longer about proving our worth to others through what we get to do.

And then one day the "whys" stop. Why has it taken so long? Why did so many revisions of that dream have to die or be rerouted all those years? For on that day a mature friend escorts you to the far back of the room, telling you only this, "We all knew this day was coming. I am so proud of you." Your friend drops you off at what looks like a train station. A fog of steam reveals only the outline of someone standing just outside an arch with the words *Dreams and Destiny* written across it.

You approach the arch and discover the figure is a Ticket Giver with one ticket in his hand. He smiles kindly and broadly, puts his hands on your shoulders, and looks into your eyes for quite a while before speaking. When he does, you suddenly realize the Ticket Giver is the same one who handed you those grace gifts all along. As he hands you the ticket, he tells you that this day was prepared before the world began. He tells you that this moment couldn't have been forced or rushed or manipulated to come one moment sooner. He tells you that he loves you as much as his Father loves him.

Then he hugs you and hands you the ticket. He tells you that this destiny was created specially for you.[12] And then he ushers you away with the words, "Now hurry up and get on that train. A whole lot of folk are waiting for you to walk into this destiny and into their lives."

And you walk through the arch into the world you were designed and prepared for. The time has come to do much of what you were placed on this earth for. You never stop returning to *The Room of Grace,* for your heart and protection reside there. But now you get to draw others to *The Room of Grace.* That's what this dream was ultimately about— your place in God's kingdom. Philip Yancey asks, "Is it absurd to believe that one human being, a tiny dot on a tiny planet, can make a difference in the history of the universe?"[13] According to the Bible, that's *exactly* how God designed the kingdom—this staging ground for the battle of the universe—to work. It's a kingdom where God uses healing and maturing people to bring his grace to hopeless and hurting people. You get to use your gifts, passion, and healed heart to show the glory of Jesus, who has loved your heart beyond telling from the beginning of time.

Kit and Bob are but two examples of individuals living out of God's dreams for them, dreams of destiny and hope. We'd like to tell you their stories so you can see what God can do with unlikely dreamers who choose to walk the path of *Trusting God* and start living in *The Room of Grace*.

Unlikely Dreamers

Kit has been called the Mother Teresa of Phoenix for her twenty-plus years of unswerving commitment to those living in the city's cycle of poverty. She now stewards a godly vision that engages the lives of hundreds who minister to thousands. Kit speaks nationally to the holistic needs of the poor, to the development of indigenous leaders, to the lifelong commitments necessary to break the cycle of poverty.

Her commitment to Christ as a teenager came in the middle of her family's greatest crisis: her mother's alcoholism and her father's suicide. A teenager from a wealthy family, Kit was immersed in the world of affluence, social standing, and notoriety. She became a debutante and prom queen. When her father died, she didn't know how to take the pain and shame anywhere but inward. As her mother's alcoholism continued to distort life, Kit learned how to form a mask to wear in her fashionably public world. She so wanted her happy-looking life to run smoothly. She wore a bright smile and a confident demeanor, but inside she was hiding and full of pain.

Her mask said, "I am competent enough." And she nearly was. Exceptionally bright and intelligent, she was mature beyond her years in many areas. In college she headed a number of campus ministries and already had a strong voice in civil rights issues. She was driven, focused, on-track, and filled with vision and immense capacity. And full of the *inevitable effects* of unresolved hurt and guilt.

Then she met Wayne. He introduced her to a family of believers who, although impressed by her talents and abilities, were committed to ministering to her person, to her heart. Despite Kit's accomplishments, her heart needed healing, her issues needing resolving, and her character needed maturing. Within this family, Kit learned the incredible principles of trust, grace, and humility. She began to trust God and others with who she was, and with their strengths to meet her needs, especially her needs for protection and love. As she began healing and maturing she also learned that her dreams were God's dreams for her. And, in time, he chose to release her into a vision even beyond her wildest dreams. She had once been a profoundly articulate influencer with an immense dream and prophetic message, headed for the "shallow grave" of disillusionment, burnout, and "train wrecks." Now she is that prophetic influencer, but protected within a community where she is trusted, known, and wonderfully loved. The results have been nothing short of breathtaking.

Kit knows that God released her into this dream, and this gives her confidence in his faithfulness to protect her in the darkest corners of the city. He provided her a place where she and others could learn through trust the incredible value of every person. It has freed her to live and minister out of who God has designed her to be.

For one day, years ago, some friends took Kit by the hand and ushered her to the far back of *The Room of Grace*. There she was handed a note by the Ticket Giver, which read: "Kit, this is what I will do with you. I will now use you to give hope to the hopeless, love to the unloved, freedom to the captives, justice to the victims. I will give you the city. Wherever you put your hand, children and adults will come to be healed and given life. I will give you land in the heart of the city and I will create a campus where people will be taught to minister to the needy. You will call it Neighborhood Ministries. Now hurry up and get on that train. A whole lot of folk are waiting for you to walk into this destiny and into their lives."

And that day, Kit fell to her knees and wept, overcome with grace and love. Overcome with a life beyond her wildest dreams. As she stood up, she looked back, smiled at the Ticket Giver, and started running to the train.

$$==\ ==$$

Bob is one of the actors, directors, and writers for a ministry that has been reaching his city through award-winning drama performed at its finest theaters. Bob also is a highly gifted songwriter who is finishing his first CD.

Most would agree, however, that he had no business coming to this place in life. Bob had violated himself and the people he loved most in this world so many times that many had given up on him. He had harbored no hope of ever being free—it seemed that he would only and always *be* what he was guilty of *doing*. Most of his Christian life Bob has been deeply troubled with some very significant and severe issues of unresolved relational sin. He has spent years in therapy. But twelve years ago, he stepped into an environment where he was, for the first time, free to be honest about who he is.

Bob actually discovered and chose to enter *The Room of Grace*. Don't be fooled. During these years, he has fallen back into the darkness of hidden duplicity more than once. But people he has grown to trust in *The Room of Grace* will not let him go. It may be hard to imagine that a person could be in *The Room of Grace* and still stumble around, failing and failed, for seasons at a time. But that is what *The Room of Grace* is all about. For God's grace is perfected in our imperfection. *The Room of Grace* is not a place where we do not sin. *The Room of Grace* is where we are protected by those who love us . . . people we have learned to trust with the deepest part of our pain, ugliness, fear, and failure.

Today, Bob understands, more than most of us, that he is a man loved by God. He now clearly trusts an identity in Christ that has become his lifeline. Yet he remains daily aware of how prone he is to engage, at any moment, in unhealthy behavior. Bob continues to struggle with sin, but when he trusted that he was actually who God said he was, he realized he could also be honest about *all* of who he is.

Finding others he could trust with himself helped Bob to experience profound healing. Now he lives in a humble realization that in spite of what is true about him, he does not have to be a victim of his own, sometimes sinful, choices. He is by faith who God says he is, even on his worst day. Yet, in his humility, he never denies that he is capable of great wrong—and he has proven this more than once in *The Room of Grace*. But Love will not let him go.

We will never forget the night Bob sang a song for John's fiftieth birthday party. That night he sat in front of eighty or so people. These were the ones Love used to bring him to a fragile but profound life of beautiful relationships and ministry, form-fitted to match his passion and gifts. Bob will always be one bad alley away from failure, but Bob is alive. God receives much glory in lives like Bob's.

Fiddling with a few notes, Bob started to sing and then abruptly stopped. He took a deep breath and then spoke to these friends words that had taken decades to form: "My friendship with you brought me into an environment where I was not discarded. I am known among this warm gathering of rabble. I am so astonished that I have been given these last few years of hope. These verses are to thank God, who has given them to me." And then he filled the night sky with this most beautiful song.

Sometimes By Faith

The morning stumbles in,
Lights a candle for the night gone by,
Rubs its weary eyes,
Wipes a tear out of the dreary skies.

Soft is the morning light, gone is the troubled night;
The dark dreams fade.
Birds in the morning sing,
A new day filtering in through the shade.

As long as dreams follow the day,
As long as light gives way to night,
God knows that you and I will walk this way:
Sometimes by faith, sometimes by sight.

When darkness settles in,
Everything we know can tend to slip away.
Things we swore we believed shiver into mist
And vanish in the gray.

The night falls hard and cold,
Dredging up all those old familiar scenes.
But look at how the morning breaks;
Think about how time can shake up everything.

As long as dreams follow the day,
As long as light gives way to night,
God knows that you and I will walk this way:
Sometimes by faith, sometimes by sight.

The morning stumbles in, lights a candle for the night gone by.
Grace draws a streak of gold across the black wall of the
eastern sky.[14]

For one day, years ago, some friends took Bob by the hand and ushered him to the far back of *The Room of Grace*. They dropped him off and said: "We all knew this day was coming. We are so proud of you." As he approached an arch with the words *Dreams and Destiny* written across it, he discovered that the figure giving out tickets was the one who handed him those grace gifts all along. That day the Ticket Giver smiled kindly and broadly on Bob, put his hands on Bob's shoulders, and looked into his eyes for quite some time. He spoke some words for only the two of them. And then he handed Bob a ticket with this written on it: "Bob, this is what I will do with you. I want you to take drama into this city. I want you to use all the gifts I've prepared in you to tell them of my love in a way they can understand. I am sending you to the Herberger Theater, the most important performing arts center in the city. Have a blast. Now hurry up and get on that train. A whole lot of folk are waiting for you to walk into this destiny and into their lives."

On that day, Bob fell to his knees and wept, overcome with grace and love. Overcome with a life beyond his wildest dreams. As he stood up, he looked back, smiled at the Ticket Giver, and started running to the train.

A New Kind of Performer

In chapter one we said: We are all performers, but because of sin we've lost confidence that we will always please our audience, and so we put on a mask. As an unintended result, no one, not even the people I love, ever get to see my true face. The real me.

We *are* all performers. One question remains: Will you perform to gain the acceptance and pleasure of your audience—and always feel that you have failed? Or will you perform out of a heart of trusting delight, knowing you have already pleased your Audience?

The offer of a life in *The Room of Grace* is not conjecture or wishful thinking. It is not religious consolation or an untried utopian state where no one lives. Many people all over this world live there. The play has been written; the good works have already been created for us to walk in.[15] We are believing who God says we are and we are actually choosing to trust it in spite of what we act out every day. We are astonished by the reality that a life beyond appearances can truly be ours. In grace, God has made it possible for us to live true-faced . . . and he is grinning widely in excited anticipation to do the same for you.

—≡ DID YOU DISCOVER?

- There is no *releasing* without *maturing*.
  There is no maturing without *healing*.
  There is no healing without *gifts of grace*.
  There are no grace gifts outside *The Room of Grace*.
  There is no *Room of Grace* without a door marked *Living Out of Who God Says I Am*, opened with a doorknob of *Humility*.
  There is no humility without choosing to walk a road called
      Trusting God.
  Only then do I learn how *God stands with me to resolve my sin*.

- In *The Room of Grace* we learn to trust, to wait, to rest in God's promises. As this causes us to grow in health and authentic relationships, we will mature toward the day of God's releasing us into our destiny.

- We—and the others in this community of grace—have taken off our masks and are learning to walk in the resplendent freedom and purposes of God.

- One of the greatest gifts we can offer another person is a safe place to fail.

- God uses suffering to mature the humble as they come under his influence and obey his truth, out of a heart of love.

- The mature influence others, not so much out of the power of their position, but out of their person.

- We learn to take responsibility for our influence.

- Life in *The Room of Grace* teaches us to wait for God's exaltation, rather than to pursue position or power.

Notes

Chapter One

1. 1 Samuel 13.
2. James 1:22-23.
3. "One who pretends to be what he is not, one who pretends to be better than he really is, to be virtuous, without really being so," *Webster's New World Dictionary* (New York: Simon & Schuster, 1996).
4. 1 Samuel 16:21; 18:8-9, 12, 15. In I Samuel 16:21 Saul loved David greatly. Once David achieves acclaim (18:8-9), Saul begins looking with suspicion on him, then progresses to fear, then to dread!
5. 1 Corinthians 6:9-11. Paul speaks of those among the Corinthian believers who were "fornicators," "idolaters," "adulterers," "effeminate," "homosexuals," on so on, and how they were "washed," "sanctified," and "justified in the name of the Lord Jesus and in the Spirit of our God." However, the important point here is that they all knew these things about themselves — each and every one of them knew the background of each and every other one! They were definitely not living in the land of doing just fine.
6. Lawrence J. Crabb, *The Pressure's Off* (Colorado Springs, Colo.: WaterBrook Press, 2000), p. 65.
7. Revelation 3:17. Some of you may be thinking, "Well, I definitely don't think we are in the Laodicean period!" Whatever your eschatological views about Revelation 2–3, please recall that the seven churches to whom John wrote on behalf of Christ himself were seven actual churches in seven actual cities in Asia Minor. The question to ask yourself is, "Do I sound like the Laodiceans with their smug self-sufficiency?"

Chapter Two

1. Romans 2:15.
2. Psalm 51:3-14.
3. Psalm 31:12; 41:7-10; 52:2-4; Proverbs 15:4; 26:28; 27:4.

4. Romans 2:15.
5. 1 Samuel 25:18-35.
6. Genesis 3:7-11.
7. Genesis 3:8-13.
8. Genesis 3:12, NASB.
9. Genesis 3:12.
10. Genesis 3:9-10, NASB.
11. 1 Samue18:8-15. Again, Saul's jealousy of David was rooted in fear. Saul saw in David the character he himself lacked; and he feared exposure by David.
12. John 5:18. The Pharisees confused their rules about the Sabbath with God's law about the Sabbath. The fact that Jesus could (and did) heal a man on the Sabbath flew in the face of their preconceived notion of what was and was not permissible on that day. Yet the evidence of the healing itself was unmistakable to them. Thus, they reacted in guilt—over their own unbelief despite overwhelming evidence—and became angry with Jesus, even to the point of wanting him dead!
13. Dallas Willard, *The Divine Conspiracy* (San Francisco: HarperSanFrancisco, 1998), pp. 150-151.

Chapter Three

1. Luke 18:9-14. The Pharisee in Jesus' story was not only unwilling to resolve the sin within him, he was, in fact, blind to it!
2. Deuteronomy 5:9. Note that it is not judgment for the iniquity that is "passed on," but the iniquity itself. The pattern of sin perpetuates itself unless we take positive steps to stop it.
3. Psalm 51:3.
4. John 3:1-2. Nicodemus came by night to Jesus, at least partly because he wanted to minimize the possibility of exposure. Interestingly, Jesus ended his conversation with Nicodemus by talking about the importance of coming to the light in order to have one's deeds vindicated (3:19-21).

Chapter Four

1. 1 Kings 22:16-18. Micaiah's prophecy was, indeed, about all of Israel and their lack of good leadership. Ahab interpreted the prophecy entirely self-centeredly: "Did I not tell you that he would not prophesy good concerning me, but evil?"
2. 1 Peter 2:21-24 and 4:19. By way of contrast, the Father was so eminently "trustable" that Christ kept entrusting himself to him, despite horrific circumstances. And he enjoins us to do the same.

3. Luke 15:11-32.
4. Matthew 23.
5. Luke 11:37-44. Jesus' condemnation of the Pharisees (and that of the lawyers that followed) was not just an expression of his disapproval of their attitudes and actions; rather it was an appeal for repentance. Otherwise, why bother to deliver it, as here, in the house of a Pharisee? The warning is "built in," as it was with Jonah's message to Nineveh: "Yet forty days and Nineveh will be overthrown." The Ninevites repented and God relented (Jonah 3:1-10).

Chapter Five

1. Matthew 5:48. See also Leviticus 19:2; Deuteronomy 18:13; 1 Peter 1:14-16.
2. Galatians 3:1-3
3. Proverbs 3:5-6.
4. Romans 5:8; Matthew 28:20b; Hebrews 13:5; Acts 18:9-10.
5. Hebrews 11:6. The word "faith" is the noun form of the word "believe" or "trust." Note the connection here.
6. Proverbs 3:5-6.
7. Philippians 3:9. Not only does it disregard the righteousness we already have in Christ, but it explicitly contradicts the principle Paul enunciates in Galatians 3:1-3 and Colossians 2:6; that is, that we received Christ by faith and that is also how we are to live in him!
8. Galatians 2:16-18, *The Message.*
9. Genesis 4:4-5. The problem was not just the offering, but something was wrong within the motive of Cain himself.
10. 1 Samuel 13:5-15; Hebrews 3:18-19; 4:2. The link between trust and obedience is unmistakable.
11. Ephesians 1:3-14.
12. I am blessed, Ephesians 1:3; I am chosen and holy, 1:4; I am adopted, 1:5; I am forgiven, 1:7; I am favored, 1:7-8; I am close to God, 2:13; I am loved, 3:17-19; I am promised great things, 3:6; I am cherished, 5:29.
13. Galatians 6:15, *The Message.*
14. Matthew 7:15-16, *The Message.*
15. Erwin McManus, *An Unstoppable Force* (Loveland, Colo.: Group Publishing, 2001), p. 156.
16. Galatians 3:5, *The Message.*
17. Revelation 3:15-22. The word in verse 16 literally is "vomit" rather than "spit," as it is often more politely translated. Politeness, however, masks God's revulsion with such lukewarm self-sufficiency!
18. Colossians 1:10-12, NASB.

19. Romans 12:1-2. Paul specifically references the truth taught earlier in this chapter in that the word he uses for "transformed" is a form of the Greek verb from which we get "metamorphosis," which is nothing other than the process of maturing into what you were designed to be!
20. Philippians 4:18.
21. 1 Thessalonians 4:1.
22. Ephesians 3:20-21.

Chapter Six
1. 1 Peter 5:5-6.
2. 1 Peter 5:5-6.
3. Galatians 5:1.
4. 2 Corinthians 12:9-10. When I recognize my own weakness, my own inability, I allow the power of Christ to be seen in me. Until I do, it is hidden by my own abilities, my own talents, my own efforts, my own pride!
5. For a more complete description of our new identity in Christ, see Henry Holloman, *The Forgotten Blessing* (Nashville: Word, 1999), chapter 3, pp. 25-40.
6. Galatians 5:1-4.
7. Deuteronomy 31:6; Hebrews 13:5.
8. Romans 8:1-4 The Law could not make us free of condemnation, for we will always fall short of it in some respect. God did make us free of condemnation, for the blood of Jesus paid for every way in which I fall short of God's character.
9. Hebrews 4:16.
10. John 1:14-18.
11. John 13:34-35.
12. J. R. R. Tolkien, *The Fellowship of the Ring* (New York: Houghton Mifflin, 1954), p. 218.
13. Romans 8:28; 1 Peter 1:3-5.
14. Galatians 5:1.
15. Psalm 78:72; Galatians 5:6,13-14; 1 Timothy 3:1-7.
16. Romans 8:28-30. God loves us so much that he wants us to be just like Jesus.
17. Jeremiah 1:5; 1 Peter 5:5-6. You may say, "But I can't be a prophet to the nations like Jeremiah!" Perhaps not, but God has plans for you that are equally stunning. See Jeremiah 29:11 and Isaiah 25:1.
18. Psalm 37:4; Proverbs 3:5-6.
19. 2 Corinthians 3:18.

Chapter Seven

1. 1 John 4:19.
2. James 2:18; 3:13. Rick Warren explains that spiritual maturity is demonstrated more by behavior than by stated beliefs. Rick Warren, *The Purpose Driven Church* (Grand Rapids, Mich.: Zondervan, 1999), pp. 336-338.
3. Genesis 2:18–3:9.
4. John 13:5-20.
5. Romans 5:5,8.
6. Zephaniah 3:17.
7. Lamentations 3:32-33. The underlying concept of *hesed* is that of "loyal love" or "covenant love." It is epitomized in Jeremiah 31:3: "I have loved you with an everlasting love; therefore I have drawn you with lovingkindness." (NASB)
8. Hebrews 12:6.
9. Psalm 33:4; 119:160; Hebrews 6:18.
10. Exodus 34:14-15; Hosea 11:1-12.
11. 1 Timothy 1:12.
12. 1 Samuel 18-19. Saul feared, and therefore mistrusted, David. Since he did not trust him, he refused the love and loyalty that David clearly offered him. Contrast this with Jonathan's willingness to trust David and the love he received—and offered—as a result.
13. Ephesians 5:21. And, according to verses 18-20, it is evidence of a Spirit-filled life.
14. *Jekyll & Hyde, The Musical,* Act One. Even those who may not know Christ understand the truth of this common grace which requires trusting relationships.
15. 1 John 4:18.
16. 2 Timothy 2:13; Deuteronomy 7:7-9. Not only will he not let us down, he cannot, because to do so would violate his very nature. He is the ultimately trustworthy one. He cannot act against his own nature since to do so would be to deny who he is—something he could never do, because he only operates in the realm of truth.
17. Isaiah 53:4-6. The ultimate grace-giver was the most beaten up of all! And in his case, he deserved none of it!
18. *Webster's New Collegiate Dictionary* (Springfield, Mass.: G&C Merriam Co., 1972).

Chapter Eight

1. Luke 18:14.
2. 1 John 1:7. The verb "cleanses" is present tense. It carries the sense of "goes on cleansing." As we walk with him in the light, his blood goes on cleansing us from all sin!
3. Isaiah 64:6. The word translated "filthy rags" (or similar phrase, depending upon the translation) is actually the word for "cast off menstrual cloths." They represented the lack of life.
4. *Webster's New Collegiate Dictionary* (Springfield, Mass.: G&C Merriam Co., 1972).
5. Colossians 2:6.
6. Titus 3:4-6.
7. 2 Corinthians 7:10-11.
8. Henry and Richard Blackaby, *Spiritual Leadership* (Nashville: Broadman & Holman, 2001), p. 237. See also Proverbs 16:18.
9. 2 Samuel 6:6-7.
10. Romans 2:4. Paul says that it is the riches of God's kindness, tolerance, and patience that lead us to repentance. Not the fear of punishment. Not self-striving. God's kindness! How sweet indeed!
11. Brennan Manning, *The Ragamuffin Gospel* (Sisters, Oreg.: Multnomah, 1990), p. 154.

Chapter Nine

1. 2 Samuel 13. Examine Absalom's response to the hurt done to his sister by Amnon: "But Absalom did not speak to Amnon either good or bad; for Absalom hated Amnon because he had violated his sister Tamar" (v. 22). Then he proceeded to plot and carry out Amnon's death! This offense also set up the heart attitude of Absalom that later issued in his rebellion against his father David.
2. Ephesians 4:32.
3. Read Jesus' astonishing words recorded in Matthew 6:12-15. He actually ties our ability to be forgiven by God to our willingness to forgive the sins of others against us! If we harbor unforgiveness in our hearts toward others, how can we even pretend that we are truly desirous of his forgiveness toward us? He has surely forgiven us of far more than we could ever be asked to forgive others of, has he not?
4. Luke 23:34.
5. C. E. MacCartney, as cited by Paul Lee Tan, ed., *Encyclopedia: Signs of the Times* (Rockville, Md.: Assurance Publishers, 1979), p. 457.

6. 1 Peter 1:7-8. If you replace the words "faith" and "believe" (as they are in most translations) with the single word "trust," you'll see the impact of this more fully.

Chapter Ten

1. Jeremiah 29:11. God delivered this promise to Israel even after seventy years of exile in Babylon! He still had remarkable plans for them. He does for you, too.
2. Matthew 3:17.
3. Hebrews 5:7-10; 1 Peter 2:21-23.
4. Philippians 2:5-11; 1 Peter 4:19.
5. Psalm 37:7; 40:4; 1 Peter 5:5-6.
6. Psalm 37:4.
7. Bruce Demarest, *Soul Guide* (Colorado Springs, Colo.: NavPress, 2003), p. 40.
8. Dallas Willard, *The Divine Conspiracy* (San Francisco: HarperSanFrancisco, 1998), pp. 353, 418.
9. Ken Gire, *Windows of the Soul* (Grand Rapids, Mich.: Zondervan, 1996), p. 217.
10. Many have benefited by placing these three phases within the timeline exercises suggested by Dr. J. Robert Clinton in *The Making of a Leader* (Colorado Springs, Colo.: NavPress, 1988) and in his other works.
11. 1 Peter 5:5-6.
12. Ephesians 2:10. God has tailor-made good works for you to perform! They're out there waiting just for you.
13. Philip Yancey, *Disappointment with God* (Grand Rapids, Mich.: Zondervan, 1988), p. 169.
14. Used with permission.
15. Philippians 1:6.

Acknowledgments

We are deeply grateful to those who in their wisdom loved us and who in their vulnerability were willing to earn our trust. For those who, in spite of what is true about us, continue to teach us about God's grace. And for those who introduced us to his dreams for our lives and now stand with us as we are privileged to share these truths with others.

Thanks to the board, staff, advisory council, and friends of Leadership Catalyst for your timeless encouragement and sacrificial investments. Special thanks go to Amanda Smith, Ellen Antill, and Mark Carver. Your "can do" spirit, skill, and friendship demonstrate why teamwork is better than solo work. We love that you are on our team!

We appreciate our dear friend, Stewart Black, a gifted theologian who expresses the message of this book through his life and teaching, and helped us clarify the biblical endnotes of *TrueFaced*.

Thanks to the men and women of Open Door Fellowship and The Neighborhood Church, with whom we are privileged to enjoy community and live in these truths.

Thanks to Alan Andrews and The Navigators National Leadership Team and many leaders, churches, and organizations who have proven the transferability of these truths during the past decade. The terrific

NavPress team cared for this project with publishing expertise, energy, and encouragement. They include Kent Wilson, Dan Rich, Terry Behimer, Toben Heim, Greg Clouse, Don Simpson, Paul Santhouse, Sarah Snelling, Monika Lewis, Candis Pflueger, Amy Slivka, Lisa Marshall, Kathleen Campbell, Jan Maniatis, and many other team members who are "difference makers." An immense debt of thanks goes to the outstanding editor NavPress secured for this project, Liz Heaney. Liz, you are a gift.

We are grateful for many volunteer readers and researchers who contributed their insights and significantly enriched this work. Deep thanks to our friends who live this message alongside us and who have given us permission to tell their stories. Finally, we would like to thank our families, who are the most loving and faithful mirrors of these truths in our lives, both when we are living in them and when we stray from them.

If you would like to know more about Leadership Catalyst, Inc. and its training programs and resources for leaders, families, organizations, institutions, and churches, please contact us at 888.249.0700 or visit our website at www.leadershipcatalyst.org.

William Thrall

Bruce McNicol

John Lynch

About Leadership Catalyst

≡ One word has the power to catalyze greatness in an individual, an organization, or a nation: *Trust.*

Surveys show that trust is the #1 requirement for influence in life and leadership. But for many, trust has been hard to come by or misplaced. There is a painful Trust Gap . . . and it appears to be widening in many arenas of the church, business, education, missions, government, and even family life.

The *mission* of Leadership Catalyst is *to build and restore trust in leaders and in those they influence.* Established in 1995, Leadership Catalyst is recognized as an international resource for helping leaders learn how to develop relationships of trust and environments of grace, which build character, authenticity, vision, and influence.

For the *individual*, Leadership Catalyst offers a variety of resource tools to help you build trust in your friendships, your family, and your community.

For the *organization*, Leadership Catalyst has designed a groundbreaking process to help leaders and teams bridge the Trust Gap. *The Catalyst Process* is a foundational, baseline process, functioning much like a computer operating system that accelerates programs in the computer.

Therefore, *The Catalyst Process* is designed to enrich and leverage the other programs that are already embraced within the organization. Delivery of *The Catalyst Process* is implemented through your organization's coaches, who are trained in Catalyst Coaches' Clinics. See the www.leadershipcatalyst.org website for details of *The Catalyst Process*.

For additional information on Leadership Catalyst and our latest resource catalog, please contact us directly.

LEADERSHIP
CATALYST

Leadership Catalyst, Inc.
Email: info@leadershipcatalyst.org
Website: www.leadershipcatalyst.org
Voice 888-249-0700 Toll-free in North America
Voice: 602-249-7000
Fax: 602-249-0611

Address:
1600 E. Northern Avenue, Suite 280
Phoenix, AZ 85020

About the Authors

BILL THRALL serves as leadership mentor for Leadership Catalyst, Inc. (LCI) and as a director on LCI's board. Prior to LCI, Bill led Open Door Fellowship in Phoenix, a church he established in 1973. Bill is also the coauthor of *The Ascent of a Leader* and *Beyond Your Best* (Jossey Bass), and continues to speak to people around the world about issues of trust, mentoring, and leadership. Bill lives in Phoenix with his wife Grace. They have three children and seven grandchildren.

BRUCE MCNICOL guides Leadership Catalyst as president, combining international work experience and degrees in finance law, and theology and organizational development. He is a respected teacher and mentor for both established and emerging leaders in multiple cultures and contexts. Also the coauthor of *The Ascent of a Leader* and *Beyond Your Best* (Jossey Bass), Bruce is active as a speaker and mentor around the world. He lives in the Phoenix area with his wife Janet and their three children.

JOHN LYNCH is a national speaker for Leadership Catalyst, Inc. John is also the teaching pastor at Open Door Fellowship, and coleads Sharkey Productions, a drama outreach in Phoenix. He is an award-winning playwright and storyteller, and lives in Phoenix with his wife and three children.